PARTNERSHIP IN THE PRIMARY SCHOOL

PARTNERSHIP IN THE PRIMARY SCHOOL

Working in collaboration

Edited by Jean Mills

London and New York

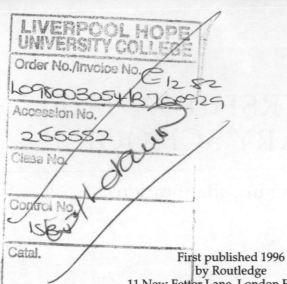
First published 1996
by Routledge
11 New Fetter Lane, London EC4P 4EE

Simultaneously published in the USA and Canada
by Routledge
29 West 35th Street, New York, NY 10001

Routledge is an International Thomson Publishing company

© 1996 Jean Mills

Typeset in Palatino by
Datix International Limited, Bungay, Suffolk
Printed and bound in Great Britain by
Clays Ltd, St. Ives PLC

British Library Cataloguing in Publication Data
A catalogue record for this book is available from the British Library

Library of Congress Cataloging in Publication Data
A catalogue record for this book has been requested

ISBN 0–415–13901–5

CONTENTS

List of contributors   vii
Acknowledgements   ix

INTRODUCTION   1
Jean Mills

Part I Whole School Approaches to Working Relationships

1 NURSERY PARTNERS   13
Jean Mills
Appendix 1: Parkway Nursery Day Plan   31
Appendix 2: Parkway Nursery Record Sheet   32

2 PLANNING IN PARTNERSHIP IN THE
  PRIMARY SCHOOL   33
Ann Lance and Anita Cliff
Appendix 1: Staff Project Questionnaire   46
Appendix 2: Structured Discussion Document   47
Appendix 3: Project Cycle   47

3 SUPPORTING PUPILS WITH SPECIAL
  EDUCATIONAL NEEDS   48
Penny Lacey

**Part II Partnership and the Curriculum: the School and
Beyond**

4 PARTNERSHIPS IN READING AND LITERACY   67
Maggie Moore

5 DEVELOPING HOME–SCHOOL LITERACY
PARTNERSHIPS IN MINORITY LANGUAGE
FAMILIES   84
Adrian Blackledge and Jamila Aljazir

6 NETWORKING IN ENVIRONMENTAL
EDUCATION   100
Mary Comber
Appendix 1: Education for Environment – School Policy
   Statement   120
Appendix 2: A Whole School Approach   122
Appendix 3: Useful Addresses   122

Part III The Shock of the New: Partnerships from Outside

7 THE PARTNERS' TALE: TEACHERS, TUTORS,
STUDENTS   125
Jean Mills
Appendix 1: Providing Support   139
Appendix 2: School Experience Competences   141

8 COLLABORATING IN ASSESSMENT: THE
OFSTED EXPERIENCE   143
Gill Hackett

Index   157

CONTRIBUTORS

Jamila Aljazir has several years' experience of working as a classroom assistant in culturally diverse settings and now, after Open University studies and teacher training, she is in her first year of teaching in an inner city school.

Adrian Blackledge taught in inner city primary schools, holding a post of responsibility for language. He is now Senior Lecturer in English at Westhill College, Birmingham and is currently carrying out research into home literacy practices in minority language families. He is author of several journal articles and editor of *Teaching Bilingual Children*, Trentham, 1994.

Anita Cliff is Curriculum Co-ordinator in a large West Midlands primary school, where she has taught for several years. She is presently a visiting teacher-fellow at the University of Central England, Birmingham.

Mary Comber is Senior Lecturer in Education at Westhill College, Birmingham, and has worked for several years on developing the science curriculum in primary schools. Author of several articles on environmental education, she recently visited several East African countries in connection with her research.

Gill Hackett taught for a number of years in West Midlands primary schools, holding posts of responsibility for language and special needs, before becoming an Advisory Teacher for Primary English. She is now Senior Lecturer in Education at Westhill College, Birmingham and PGCE Programme Leader.

Penny Lacey initially taught in Key Stage 1 mainstream and then children with learning difficulties in special education. She has been in Higher Education for five years and is currently Lecturer in Education at Birmingham University. She is co-author, with Jenny Lomas, of, *Support Services and the Curriculum: A Practical Guide to Collaboration*, David Fulton, 1993. Her present research is on multi-disciplinary teams in the education service.

Ann Lance spent twenty years teaching in inner city primary schools, including nine as a Headteacher. This was followed by a period of secondment to the National Primary Centre. She is currently Senior Lecturer in Education at Westhill College, Birmingham and editor of the NPC journal, *Primary Practice*.

Jean Mills has taught since the 1970s in nursery, infant and junior schools in England and lectured in Higher Education in Canada and Australia. Author/Editor of several articles on Primary Education and books, including *Bilingualism in the Primary School*, Routledge, and *Primary School People*, Routledge (both with Richard W. Mills), she was formerly Deputy of the Language Support Service in a large Local Authority. She is currently Head of Education Studies, Westhill College, Birmingham.

Maggie Moore is currently Senior Lecturer in Education at Newman College, Birmingham, having had substantial teaching experience in primary schools, and in special needs education. She has written widely on special needs and also on reading, including (with Barrie Wade) *Supporting Readers: School and Classroom Strategies*, David Fulton, 1995. Also a children's author, she is currently researching into children's early literacy, having written a thesis on reading for her doctorate.

ACKNOWLEDGEMENTS

I wish to record my special thanks to my contributor colleagues for their committed and conscientious involvement and to Westhill College and my colleagues in the Education Department for their support and help during my sabbatical term in 1995, during which I collected the data and wrote my chapters for this book. I am also very grateful for the generous help given by the headteachers and staff who allowed my research and that of my contributors to be conducted in their schools and classrooms and gave their time so willingly. My thanks are also due to all past and present members of the PITPE (Partnership in Training in Primary Education) team and associated colleagues at Westhill College. Thanks particularly to Shirley Mercer, School Liaison Tutor, for permission to reproduce the *School Experience Competences*, and to Julie Fox for permission to quote her.

Parts of Chapters 2 and 6 are based on material that has appeared in *Primary Practice*, the journal of the National Primary Centre, and are reproduced with the kind permission of the editor, Ann Lance.

In accordance with accepted practice, identities of individuals and institutions have generally been disguised. Two schools are, however, identified in Chapter 6, and Mary Comber would like to thank the headteachers, Lorna Field and Chris Leach, and Scott Sinclair of the DEC (Development Education Centre), Selly Oak, Birmingham for his help and permission to reproduce *A Whole School Approach*.

Finally, this book is dedicated to my dear husband, Richard, for all his many qualities (and never a cross word. Well, hardly ever).

INTRODUCTION

Jean Mills

> The term 'partnership' is set to become the buzzword for the nineties.
>
> (Family Rights Group, 1991)

This book has been written as a companion to *Primary School People: Getting to Know Your Colleagues*, Routledge, 1995. That volume explored some of the key roles of the various adults who work in schools with class teachers, but are not necessarily in partnership with them. This one approaches the same situation from another angle: significant scenarios in which partnership work appears in schools and the principles that support it.

However, before we move on to the different contributions, it is useful to reflect on the partnership phenomenon and its significance. As the quotation above indicates, since it was written in the context of social work and the Children Act, 1989, 'partnership' is a notion that appears in many areas of social and political debate, not just in education. Indeed, the Labour Party Education Policy document published in June 1995, was entitled *Diversity and Excellence. A New Partnership for Parents*.

Why is there this emphasis? Is it a *fin de siècle* spasm, in which the greedy, grasping, individualistic 1980s are being replaced by the caring, community oriented 1990s? Or are there, in fact, larger forces at work that are propelling us into these relationships?

In educational contexts several overlapping circumstances appear to lie behind this development and what Hargreaves has called 'the new professionalism' (quoted in Fish, 1995: 187). These are:

- the greater involvement of parents in their children's education in school;

1

- the increasing number of adults other than teachers in class-rooms; and
- the effects of recent legislation and government policies.

As will be seen, these different categories are inter-related, but all contribute to the changing pattern of classroom work.

PARENTAL INVOLVEMENT

The roots of parental involvement can be traced back over thirty years. Both Newsom (Central Advisory Council for Education, 1963) and Plowden (DES, 1967) indicated the official acceptance of the importance of involving parents in their children's schooling. Indeed Plowden included a chapter entitled 'Participation by Parents' and proposed that schools should develop policies whereby:

- the head and class teacher should meet parents before a child enters school;
- there should be regular open days and private meetings;
- parents should receive school booklets and annual written reports; and
- schools should be used by the community.

These radical, yet common-sense, proposals appear as a basic entitlement to us today.

Since that time, of course, links with parents have developed considerably, and the very term 'parental involvement' now covers a range of scenarios from helping on the school trip, and working alongside a teacher in a curriculum area, to systematic participation in programmes that aim to raise children's achievement. Such initiatives have been supported by materials which recognised that schools needed guidance in developing these kinds of whole school approaches (Long, 1983; Bastiani, 1989; Docking, 1990). Furthermore, it has been noted that these scenarios reflect different models, from the 'top down' version, with professionals controlling and organising parents, to more community oriented versions in which parents are involved in management and decision making and where their expertise is recognised (Tizard *et al.*, 1981: 4). It is argued that the latter model, with its emphasis on two-way communication and what parents have to offer in terms of knowledge and skills, is more effective in creating partnerships (Powell, 1995: 104).

OTHER ADULTS

As well as parents in their classrooms, teachers now work along-side an increasing range of other professionals. These may include:

- colleagues in a team-teaching situation;
- peripatetic teachers for English as a second language or special needs;
- home–school liaison teachers;
- integration/welfare/classroom assistants;
- speech and physiotherapists;
- educational psychologists; and
- Reading Recovery teachers.

In particular, the Warnock Report, (DES, 1978) (which also emphasised the importance of treating parents as equal partners) and the 1981 Education Act provided the impetus for the employment of integration assistants.

> The picture of classrooms containing two, three or even more adults working together, represents a major departure from the stereotype of the classroom (one adult to one class) which the public probably holds.
>
> (Thomas, 1992: 3)

These increasing numbers have brought with them the realisation that roles and relationships may need to be reappraised for all parties to work harmoniously and effectively together. As Thomas (1992: 2) notes, the team-teaching initiatives of the 1960s 'atrophied due to inadequate attention to the working of the team'. Balshaw (1991) cites the dissatisfactions of a group of special needs support assistants that may be the shared experience of many of the adults cited earlier. These included: insufficient time for preparation and evaluation with individual teachers; arriving to find the teacher unprepared and having to fit in as well as possible; being unsure about roles and responsibilities; needing training in some areas; having too much time taken with menial tasks.

Significantly, the National Foundation for Educational Research produced partnership teaching materials to support teachers in multilingual classrooms, noting that,

> Most local education authorities have accepted the policy of providing language support for bilingual pupils within the mainstream classroom. . . . However, language support

within the mainstream has implications for classroom teaching styles and organisational strategies, and also for traditional school structures, if it is to be effective.

(Bourne and McPake, 1991: 7).

In other words, productive ways of capitalising on these significant human resources need to be employed, and, if necessary, as these authors stress, there should be in-service training. It is not just, as a student wrote in her school evaluation, 'a matter of common sense really'. As with the models of parental involvement, proposed solutions, notably by the authors cited above, emphasise an ideology that is committed to sharing the classroom; involves all participants in the formulation of whole school policies; ensures open discussion of concerns and expectations; builds in clear task and role definition; enables joint planning, focusing on individuals' strengths and weaknesses, and regular, formalised evaluation (Bourne and McPake, 1991: 14; Thomas, 1992: 204).

GOVERNMENT INITIATIVES

Several Acts of Parliament, of which the 1981 Education Act was an early example, have served to strengthen the impetus towards educational collaboration. For example, as David (1994: xv) notes, the Children Act 1989 made it obligatory for 'the different agencies within local authorities and the community and voluntary organisations [to] work together to provide effective services for children and their families'. Both the 1986 Education Act (which gave parents a greater role in schools' governing bodies) and the 1988 Act reflected the government's ideology of giving more power to parents. The trend has been to increase parental rights over choice of school; representation on governing bodies; and receipt of information from schools. At the time of writing this shows no sign of abating. In certain instances this tendency appears to be entangled with a view of parents as consumers in the education market, as evidenced by discussions such as those on the provision of nursery vouchers.

Such a view would seem at odds with the notion of a partnership role. Indeed, some government documents do not appear to have resolved this inconsistency. The Parents' Charter (DES, 1991) outlines parents' rights and then goes on to say:

4

This charter will help you to become a more effective partner in your child's education. As a partner you have important responsibilities. . . . Your child's education is your
concern and you will want to play your full part at every
stage.

(DES, 1991: 1)

The biggest help you can give to your child is to show that
you are interested and see the value of what he or she is
doing at school. Such support can have a real effect on your
child's performance.

(DES, 1991: 19)

Ironically, this is what appears to have occurred in many instances. Policies which were designed to put pressure on schools
to respond to parental concerns and to transfer some of their
powers, while undoubtedly doing just that, have also increased
parental knowledge about their internal workings; the constraints
they operate within; and boosted the sense of identification with
particular institutions. Rather than blaming the local school,
which they now help to run, for deficiencies, the protests about
budget cuts during 1995 suggest that many parents now blame
the government. Parents and schools have moved closer together
in many cases.

A similar irony has appeared as a result of government requirements for teacher educators to transfer more training into
schools (DFE, 1992, 1993). Far from a stampede occurring
whereby schools swiftly set up their own school-based courses,
both schools and colleges have realised that mutual support is
needed in such an enterprise. Schools cannot take the whole
burden overnight. Colleges have expertise to offer schools. The
evidence appears to be that both build on an existing relationship,
move closer together and in the process open up their practice to
each other.

In short, there is evidence of a mismatch between intention and
outcome. At the same time there have been other effects on the
culture of schools. Several commentators have noted 'the potentially manipulative function of recent encouragement to be col-
legial' (Acker, cited by Biott and Easen, 1994: 119). Thus, teachers
are not only required formally to work together on the School
Development plan, assessment frameworks, planning and the
writing of policies, they actually 'interpret the demands of the

ERA collectively to help each other to cope creatively and to develop sensible ways of doing what is now expected of them' (Biott and Easen, 1994.). Similarly, Brighouse and Moon (1990) note, 'the National Curriculum demands a whole school approach and can be used to develop the capacity of teachers to act as a team'. Moreover, as Biott and Easen point out, this way of working is more likely to be successful in schools where there is already an established philosophy of collaborative work, underpinned by formal and informal structures, both between teachers and between children. These schools already have that sense of community and interdependence that Nias (1989) has termed 'the culture of collaboration'. Schools which have such a culture are depicted in Chapters 1 and 2.

In reviewing all of these impulses it would seem that teachers are in the grip of what Skilbeck has defined as 'the partnership trend which emphasises the role of the teacher as a partner and co-operative worker' (quoted in Fish, 1995: 186). It is this feature in particular that Hargreaves has designated 'the new professionalism', noted earlier, and characterised as meaning 'closer, more collaborative relationships with colleagues, students, parents, involving more explicit negotiation of roles and responsibilities' (quoted in Fish, 1995: 187). Hargreaves also charts the development of this new role in terms of trends, including the following:

- from hierarchies to teams: in which . . . because of the reforms, and the need for a vast range of functions to be carried out, everyone has a leadership role to play
- from liaison to partnership: in which the relationship between lecturers and mentors has changed, and where practising teachers will contribute more to design and planning of courses, be trained . . . and share in assessment,
- from survivalism to empowerment: in which the structures that nourish the new professionalism are also, by mistake as it were, empowering schools and teachers.

(Hargeaves, quoted in Fish, 1995: 188)

Moreover, as was noted at the beginning of this chapter, such trends are by no means limited to education. Elliott notes that this different professional image is evolving in other professions, such as social work and the law, along with 'collaboration with clients in identifying and clarifying their problems; the importance of communication and empathy with clients' (quoted in Fish, 1995).

PARTNERSHIP RELATIONSHIPS

These, then, appear to be some of the forces that are propelling teachers into working with others collaboratively and in teams. Obviously, not all situations will involve partnership relationships. As Thomas (1992: 2) shows, members of teams can work together, but neither recognise that they are in a team situation nor employ successful strategies. The term itself suggests a hierarchy. Similarly, formal requirements to work collaboratively 'may . . . involve working with others merely to fulfil a sense of duty. We might refer to this as "contractual membership"' (Biott and Easen, 1994: 110).

However, there are now a variety of joint working situations that are called 'partnerships'. In Chapter 3 Penny Lacey describes the different working relationships (such as networks and teams, and the skills of liaising and collaborating) that may be covered by this broad term. A random sample of my own has discovered the following projects that have employed it:

- collaboration between secondary and linked primary schools to provide continuity between age phases;
- links between a hospital school and local primary schools to improve inter-agency support;
- closer working relationships between a special school and mainstream schools;
- developing teamwork in an infant school to teach science in Key Stage 1;
- a group of primary schools co-ordinating their approach to baseline assessment; and
- nursery schools sharing procedures in identifying and monitoring special needs.

This book will describe several more examples.

What features do these situations have in common that warrant the designation 'partnership'? Is the term set to become an educational cliché, an unsubstantiated euphemism for any relationship of two or more people in a school context? As we have seen before in education, when an innovation becomes associated with a catch phrase (such as 'progressive', 'mixed ability', 'team-teaching', 'real reading') either a distorted interpretation becomes rife or the label is applied indiscriminately to inappropriate situations. For, in Bloom's memorable dictum, 'In education we continue to be seduced by the equivalent of snake-oil remedies, fake cancer cures, perpetual motion contraptions, and old wives' tales, Myth and reality are not clearly differentiated, and we frequently prefer the former to the latter' (quoted in Bennett, 1976: 1).

The development of parental involvement in the 1980s prompted De'Athe and Pugh (1984: 85) to define the fundamental principle behind a true partnership as 'sharing; a sharing of knowledge, of power, of resources, of information, of expertise, of experience and decision making', which might involve the need for 'professionals to rethink their roles and perhaps act as a catalyst, enabler, or supporter rather than the teacher, healer or fixer of problems'. Several of these qualities will be in evidence in the case studies that follow, which will also serve to augment and enhance this definition.

The book is divided into three parts. Part I examines the way a whole school operates as a team in terms of school development, curriculum planning, collaborative relationships, links with the community, considering first the nursery school approach (Chapter 1, Jean Mills) and then that of the primary school (Chapter 2, Ann Lance and Anita Cliff). In Chapter 3 classroom teams which involve teachers and SEN support assistants are discussed by Penny Lacey.

Part II considers the ways in which the curriculum (and consequently children's learning) is enhanced and developed by different types of partnerships. In the familiar area of literacy these can operate within schools (Chapter 4, Maggie Moore), and between schools and children's homes (Chapter 5, Adrian Blackledge and Jamila Aljazir). In the less familiar area of environment education it can be argued that a network of relationships is essential (Chapter 6, Mary Comber).

Finally Part III reviews formal partnerships which are developing as a direct result of government requirements, firstly between schools and Higher Education (Chapter 7, Jean Mills), and secondly within the new OFSTED teams (Chapter 8, Gill Hackett).

The intention is that by exploring all of these particular instances, not only will the key attributes of partnership relationships be exposed but readers will be able to relate these to their own situation, either to develop practice or as an articulation of the familiar.

REFERENCES

Balshaw, M. (1991) *Help in the Classroom*, London: David Fulton.

Bastiani, J. (1989) *Working with Parents*, Windsor: NFER-Nelson.

Bennett, N. (1976) *Teaching Styles and Pupil Progress*, London: Open Books.

Biott, C. and Easen, P. (1994) *Collaborative Learning in Staffrooms and Classrooms*, London: David Fulton.

Bourne, J. and McPake, J. (1991) *Partnership Teaching: An In-Service Pack for Schools*, London: HMSO

Brighouse, T. and Moon, B. (1990) *Managing the National Curriculum*, London: Longman.

Central Advisory Council for Education (1963) *Half Our Future* (Newsom Report), London: HMSO.

David, T. (1994) *Working Together for Young Children*, London: Routledge.

De'Athe, E. and Pugh, G. (1984) *Working Together: Parents and Professionals as Partners*, Partnership Paper 1, London: National Children's Bureau.

DES (Department of Education and Science) (1967) *Children and Their Primary Schools* (Plowden Report), London: HMSO.

DES (1978) *Special Educational Needs. Report of the Committee of Enquiry into the Education of Handicapped Children and Young People* (Warnock Report), London: HMSO.

DES (1991) *The Parents' Charter: You and Your Child's Education*, London: HMSO.

DFE (Department for Education) (1992) *Initial Teacher Training (Secondary Phase) (Circular 9/92)*, London: DFE.

DFE (1993) *The Initial Training of Primary School Teachers: New Criteria for Courses (Circular 14/93)*, London: DFE.

Docking, J. (1990) *Primary Schools and Parents*, London: Hodder and Stoughton.

Fish, D. (1995) *Quality Mentoring for Student Teachers*, London: David Fulton.

Long, R. (1983) *Developing Parental Involvement in Primary Schools*, London: Macmillan.

Mills, J. and Mills, R.W. (1995) *Primary School People. Getting to Know Your Colleagues*, London: Routledge.

Nias, J. (1989) *Primary Teachers Talking: A Study of Teaching as Work*, London: Routledge.

Powell, J. (1995) 'The work of a home–school liaison teacher', in J. Mills, and R.W. Mills (eds) *Primary School People*, London: Routledge.

Thomas, G. (1992) *Effective Classroom Teamwork*, London: Routledge.

Tizard, B., Mortimore, J. and Burchell, B. (1981) *Involving Parents in Nursery and Infant Schools: A Source Book for Teachers*, London: Grant McIntyre.

Part I

WHOLE SCHOOL APPROACHES TO WORKING RELATIONSHIPS

1

NURSERY PARTNERS

Jean Mills

This opening chapter deliberately focuses on nursery education, not just because there is increasing discussion of provision for under-fives by politicians and the media, nor because a nursery may be the first experience for a child of formal education. It is primarily because, by the nature of their organisation, nurseries, often provide models for working in partnership both within the school and beyond. Thus, this section is presented as a microcosm for the rest of the book. Here there will be a description of a range of initiatives and patterns of working that exist within (arguably) the smallest unit in the school system. Later in the book the focus will be on separate issues in separate schools.

Secondly, nurseries operated in teams long before it was common practice in primary schools. Within a relatively small physical environment, they involve a range of adults, including teachers, nursery nurses, students on placement and outside professionals, who cannot fail to be aware of each other's practice and the need to work co-operatively. What does this mean for different nurseries? How does a headteacher capitalise on these kinds of demands for the benefit of the children? What are the implications for relationships with parents, and others outside the school? At this point let us turn to Parkway Nursery School and to see how one institution and its headteacher, Mrs Andrews, has met these challenges.

PARKWAY NURSERY SCHOOL

Parkway is a seventy place (or unit) nursery school in an inner city area of a large city. It is housed in a modern, purpose-built building, surrounded by grassy open spaces, post-war council

13

housing, maisonettes and high-rise flats, many of which are undergoing refurbishment through the city's urban regeneration project. The population is culturally diverse, with white, some Asian, but mainly Afro-Caribbean families living in the area. Nearby, are various factories in which some of the children's families work. Some other families experience the stress of poverty and unemployment.

The school itself is open plan, with three large interlinked classrooms, each served by a teacher and a nursery nurse; a large community room for parents, meetings and other activities; and a kitchen to prepare the children's midday meal. The non-teaching head (more of that later) has been at the school for twelve years and is supported by a deputy, and six members of staff. These, then, are the apparently incidental details of the school, some of which will have significance later. As a setting for partnership, how does it operate and what are the key elements that underpin those partnerships?

Inside the school: partnership in planning

The first feature I am going to highlight is the coherence and quality of the planning that takes place. For most schools the headteacher is a crucial figure. As Acker noted 'headteachers were pivotal in building and maintaining a culture of collaboration which was essentially about personal relationships' (quoted in Biott and Easen, 1994: 119). Parkway is no different. The headteacher here, along with her staff, as she emphasises, has developed the framework within which they can plan and work. Overall, this framework emphasises inclusiveness, responsibility, ownership and communication. The formal, concrete aspects of it are realised by their written planning, which reflects the collaborative ethos of the school, I feel, more than a response to 'teachers' formal obligations to work together on such things as curriculum review and the writing of annual school development plans' as a result of the 1988 Education Act (Biott and Easen, 1994: 71).

Planning at Parkway stems from the writing of the School Development Plan and inclusiveness is reflected by the fact that, all staff have a part in this. Truly, small is beautiful when there is the opportunity to involve everyone in the school's development. Thus, in the initial stages, during a staff meeting every member is given a questionnaire to complete showing where they feel the school is in its development, immediate targets, and how these might be achieved. This includes such questions as:

- Do you feel your responsibilities are clear? Would you like any change in your role?
- What are the interesting parts of your work?
- In what areas do you think you need more experience?
- Are you experiencing any frustrations or problems in your post?
- How do you think we might prepare for your long-term future?

(The questionnaire is derived from the GRIDS approach to school review and development, Abbott, *et al.*, 1988.) Achievements for the previous year are then discussed. This is followed by individual interviews with the head.

While the previous discussions have been open, the interview is confidential, since part of the overall planning will take into consideration who staff prefer to work with and what they would like to change. From the head's point of view, 'it's left to me as the leader, if you like, to try to make things work. There are always hiccups in any staff. I try to make sure everyone is happy with what's going on, so the interview is totally confidential. It doesn't work if that's open, it upsets people, but the GRIDS are open.' The questionnaires are collated along with the feedback from the interviews and areas for development are focused on. For example, this year these were: writing schemes of work for role play, drama and language; reviewing equipment; updating job descriptions; reviewing pupil records, working with other agencies. The criteria for success were agreed as, among others: the whole staff collaborating in writing the schemes; the production of a general list of equipment; each staff member meeting the head to review responsibilities; new record sheets being used consistently by all staff; greater awareness of the childcare strategy in the community.

The formulation of policies involves a similar corporate effort based on staff discussion. The head notes, 'it involves the actual ethos of the place in the sense that the staff formulate the policy, it's not me that writes them. If it's about something that's happening already, say special needs, I will ask the special needs teacher to write down what she does. Rather than me formulating the policy it's actually what happens here then . . . and if we need to change that comes up as a discussion with the whole staff.'

A record of staff meetings ensures that absent staff keep up with events. For example, on one particular day these were: the developments in each classroom; what activities should take place in the morning session; how planning and topic sheets would be drawn up; what kinds of records would be used, how they would be completed. Similarly, when members of staff receive any training outside school they complete an evaluation form so that a record is kept of what has been useful, as had happened recently for a first aid course, one on the science curriculum, and the Code of Practice for Special Needs. These might then be followed by an in-service session on this area for the rest of the staff. Awareness of accountability means that while most communication is oral, written evidence is constantly compiled.

Termly and half-termly curriculum planning occurs in common with other schools, as does joint planning by teachers and nursery nurses, working to a topic or theme and covering areas of experience. For example, a topic web on 'Carnivals' included:

- Science: tasting foods and recording; cooking Afro-Caribbean food with parent helpers (soup, dumplings, fritters);
- Literacy: *Nini at Carnival*; *Anansi*; a calypso alphabet;
- Art: papier mâché masks; face painting;
- Music: salsa, calypso, reggae.

The themes are written up for all staff, and copied so that everyone knows what is happening elsewhere. On their planning sheets staff have a list of the areas they have chosen to focus on as an *aide-mémoire*: Art, Music, PE, Literacy, Language, Drama, Turntaking, Fine Motor, Technology, IT, Maths, and Science. These roughly follow the areas covered by the OFSTED guidelines for inspection of nursery schools: Social, Linguistic, Physical, Mathematical, Science, Technology, Aesthetic, Creative.

For Parkway, with its open plan design, there is a further factor, consistency on a daily basis. Again, this requires communication. So, on Thursday lunchtimes each team plans in detail for the following week, and all staff then get a plan of the activities in each room in one day, as in Appendix 1. 'It makes sense, for example, if you've got waterplay at one end it would be nice to have colour in it or different equipment so it's floating and sinking. So you've got a spread of activities throughout the nursery.' These are also monitored on a weekly basis, so that, for example, a check can be kept on the amount of maths taking place.

This communication is also needed in record keeping. Since the children are not confined to one classroom, the activities they experience with an adult need to be monitored. So each member of staff has an alphabetical list of the children and a tick chart of the areas of experience. Each child's experiences are recorded and each half term the ticks are collated and matched to the child's attendance. The record can show, for example, that Tyler has mainly done art (26 ticks); Russell, in contrast has done art once, but only attended 15 sessions; Naomi has done no art, but has not been arriving until 10.30, by which time it has been cleared away. As it is colour coded according to the classroom the child was in, the record also shows how much the children move around, indicating their sociability and adventurousness. 'It's our way of making sure we don't lose the children. You wouldn't necessarily need this in every set up.'

Again, the head is the linch pin for evaluation and record keeping.

Each half term I do records with each member of staff. They talk to me about each child and I keep a profile and have this collated so I know what they've done. We're about to trial a new set of records and will highlight the statements and put comments on for each child. The staff have worked this out, it isn't me. When they evaluate how the week's gone to feedback to me it goes back in the file. It gives them an idea of what they've covered and what they need to cover for another week.

(The headings on the record sheet are included in Appendix 2.)

Relationships

What should also have become clear in this description is the other key element without which this type of planning and record keeping would not function so efficiently: that is, the nature of the relationships. For me, this was encapsulated on one of my visits by the large group photograph of the staff by the main door. Many schools, of course, have separate photographs of their personnel in their entrances. In this picture, however, the staff were presented as a unit, named but without their status indicated. Yet more evidence of what has been called a 'flat hierarchy' (Yeomans, quoted in Biott and Easen, 1994: 73). It is my experience that on entering a nursery, in particular, it is not always immediately obvious who is a teacher, nursery nurse or parent, so similar are their working interactions with the children.

At Parkway this is deliberate. Here is the head's view of that policy:

> With new parents when I introduce them to members of staff I do not say their rank. I don't make a hierarchy decision at all, I have to be asked if they want something specifically, who is the special needs teacher, for instance. I basically don't tell anyone who is who. Now I think that is quite important because it gives the ground work philosophy to every member of staff, they are all a member of staff. It's harder running a school like this being totally democratic and having me as the lead at times, than having a hierarchical system. This gives power and responsibility to people and sometimes that power can be abused. But it can also be extremely rewarding because people come up with things. They're doing a whole thing on dance this term. I've had nothing to do with it. It doesn't have to be a nursery nurse or a teacher, it's whoever's interested. For instance, in our industry links it has all been the nursery nurses and they have been the ones who have gone out and monitored a half day session and then taken groups of children to visit. As far as I'm concerned I'm quite happy with that. All staff are involved on new parents afternoons. It can be nursery nurses, it can be teachers taking the admission details.

This is not to say that staff do not have defined roles and areas of responsibility. Mrs Andrews reflected on her own role thus: 'I'm not a teaching head, that isn't the role the staff want me to play. My role will be observing staff; supporting staff; congratulating staff, because people do not get the pats on the back that they need ... nice things as well as criticism.' Similarly, for the deputy the role has developed over time as 'it can be that the deputy's role gets almost lost over time if you're not careful'. Thus, the deputy oversees all in-service training, absences, phoning for cover, liaison with local playgroups, and planning, while the head writes the final version of policies after staff contributions.

Obviously, though, things are not going to run smoothly all the time, and some problems can be aired during the confidential discussion. An 'open door' policy is also part of this approach: 'I'd rather people just walked in when they're upset about something, because someone from the outside can make you look at something totally differently. This has grown over time. It isn't easy and it's one of the things that some members of staff find easier than others.'

There are also particular issues of staff relationships related to the 'flat hierarchy' that present themselves in a nursery. One of these is the differential between teachers and nursery nurses. During their working day these two professionals may be carrying out very similar tasks and, as we have seen, taking on important responsibilities, yet they have quite different training and qualifications, and, potentially a sore point, a different salary. As this nursery acknowledges this can be a difficult issue, which is partly accommodated by the monitoring interview and the policy of changing rooms (and possibly partners) every year. Similarly, in the light of the job description review, staff had collectively reallocated responsibilities so that each person now covered an area they were interested in or wanted to know more about. Ultimately, however, whatever the daily routine, it is the teachers who take on the responsibility for resolving problems, and I know from my own experience that it is the teacher concerned who would mediate if, for example, a student teacher on placement and a nursery nurse did not get on.

A further issue, again related to the roles undertaken in this setting, is that of career development. The nursery nurses in particular, invariably go for promotion, but have often become so experienced and knowledgeable that they can appear threatening in another setting. Consequently, they tend to find promotion in other team situations, especially in special schools or social services, for example, running a family centre. In common with many organisations, references are open, and staff, in discussion with the head, are invited to suggest anything they feel might be added.

Parents

Parents have already been mentioned several times in passing, and again it has been my experience to arrive in the middle of a science open day to find parents, staff, students and children are all involved in workshops and activities in all parts of the nursery. Significantly, also, the head's room looks out to the main entrance where she can see all arrivals, and they can see her. It is common, when sitting in the head's room, to see parents waving to her as they drop their children, or for her to jump up to tap the window because she wants a quick word.

The school's policy states:

> Parents are made welcome at any time; we feel staff and parents are partners in the children's education. Being a nursery we only have families with us for a short time, and it can take six months to one year for parents to get used to us and trust us. The head teacher has an 'open door' policy. Parents seeking advice are helped as much as possible. We have some parents who still come to coffee mornings and events even though their children have left. We also encourage parents to seek training and employment, taking jobs within the school, whenever possible.

The requirement of the Children Act 1989 to work in partnership with parents was already well established at Parkway.

Ideally, then, the communication and support is two way. Parents, as in many schools, will pass on sensitive information and need to know that confidentiality is respected. For example, a mother may not want everyone to know why she does not want her child's father to collect him. Staff may find themselves in a counselling role, to the extent that, in the light of a particular situation, the head had been urged by the others to attend a bereavement counselling course. At the same time, the extensive record keeping means that staff can respond to parents' queries and concerns by showing them their child's records, and, for special needs children, can support parents by, after discussion, writing their responses for them during statementing procedures. A staff member was supporting parents in running the parent's childcare library (topics include a death in the family; coping with bedwetting), and the toy library.

On the other hand, parents support the school on social occasions, such as the popular parents' disco and the Mothers' Day party; in fund raising (the sponsored toddle in aid of Leukaemia Care) and open days. A working party of parents this year had written the new school booklet, and, interestingly, were prepared to be more prescriptive than the staff in citing 'Do's and Don'ts'.

This was resolved as, 'Things to Remember', which was felt to be more positive but still useful for new parents. A group was now working on a leaflet with the community education development officer, 'How to help your child to learn'. Similarly, during the annual staff and children holiday on a farm, parents volunteer to work in the nursery to ease staffing problems, or, indeed, to stay at the farm with their children.

Outside the school: community links

Schools

Parents, of course, are one bridge with the outside world. There are, however, many more. For instance, all the local schools (two nursery, six primary and one secondary) work as a group. The headteachers have four 8.00 a.m. and two afternoon meetings per term and work to a shared development plan. They were now lucky enough to have a retired headteacher working for them for two days a week to implement some of their plans. This year one of the targets had been attendance, so a leaflet was produced for all the schools along with a shared letter (headed Parkway Schools) to put over a coherent philosophy. Similarly, Mrs Andrews holds the area's central waiting list of nursery places and knows, for example, if parents have registered at five primary schools. The schools can then be informed and know that they cannot guarantee to fill all their places, which helps their administration. In support, the group had bought her a fax machine.

The nursery heads in the city also work together (at present on delegation of school budgets) and meet twice a term. Recently, Parkway had also been involved with two other city nursery schools on a project funded by the National Primary Centre on special educational needs and assessment. As a result students from a sixth form college had taken culturally appropriate photographs in the nursery, made them into jigsaws, and would be returning to complete their project by playing with the jigsaws with the children. At another level, the nursery children will be visiting an urban farm with children from the nearest primary school and joining in a shared reading programme.

The education authority itself can also provide support in addition to its normal role of providing central services, such as the educational psychologists. Recently, for example, the school had the opportunity to bid for an artist in residence. As the school development plan had highlighted art this was an ideal opportunity. It also meant that the deputy had a prominent role in writing the bid. Again in discussion, the staff favoured a young male Afro-Caribbean artist for the very positive image he would give to many of the children. Over a fortnight the artist worked in every room teaching the children to take photographs of themselves, to do pastel drawings, and in turn producing lovely drawings of them.

Agencies

Naturally, there are other agencies that are essential to the children's welfare, and there is a close relationship with social services. The local office had, in fact, asked to send their staff to the nursery's in-service meetings, and had passed on their record sheet as an aid to greater consistency. As a result of these contacts a three day in-service programme on language and special needs had taken place at Parkway with all the local nurseries, nursery classes, day nurseries and social services represented. One of Parkway's nursery nurses was now doing outreach work with all of the participants from the course to carry on its work, finding which children in the area needed language support, and helping individual schools to provide that help.

In addition, all the services which work in the area for the under-fives meet together as the Child Care Strategy Committee. Besides schools these include: Barnardo's, latchkey services, play schemes and community childminders. The Committee was focusing (as above) on in-service training across agencies and departments for under-fives' workers and volunteers. Social services day nurseries, for example, were receiving good training on child protection but found it difficult to have anything on the curriculum.

A further target for the school was a closer relationship with the health authority. Although the local health visitors are known, and are very busy, there is no school nurse (the school is non-statutory provision). In addition, the school feels a lack of contact and feedback from the dental services, hearing, speech therapy, paediatricians and child psychologists (as distinct from the educational psychologists). Consequently, initially the head had asked to attend the monthly meetings in the area to get her, the nursery and what it has to offer known by these other professionals. As David (1994: xv) notes, it is essential that 'the different agencies within local authorities and the community and voluntary organisations . . . work together to provide effective services for children and their families' and this has been reinforced by the Children Act, 1989.

Industry

In this geographical area the notion of the local community is wide and has also been taken to include those who work there. As an initiative by the local heads group, Mrs Andrews was asked to put on a conference for industry at a local company, Sayco. There were, initially, several motives. For the secondary schools it was finding work experience placements and careers education. For the primary schools, it was felt that generally the children were uninformed about job possibilities, and Mrs Andrews felt that 'my children are so open they would learn a lot very quickly and industry would learn what we are about in nursery education'. The companies, in turn, were curious about the schools, and the schools felt they could gain from them, for instance, in terms of less vandalism. (This has proved to be the case, and involving secondary pupils in the nursery had a similar effect: 'If you involve people you get respect'.) After the conference different schools and companies teamed up on different projects.

Parkway's first link was with the local dairy. 'To the children milk arrives on your doorstep or you buy it in the supermarket.' The discoveries that surprised them on their visits included: 'the smell, especially the disinfectant. How you had to wear protective clothing and helmets and how a number of the children's relatives worked there. They had no idea that's what they did. They went to work and just disappeared out of the children's lives.' In return the children are going back to the dairy to plant out a tub of plants for their foyer to say thank you.

The education authority then asked Parkway to receive six industrialists. As the topic at the time was, 'The Little Red Hen', on the day of the visit each nursery room prepared a different activity. The dairy man brought milk and cheeses; a little red hen was brought in and set up in one of the areas; outside was a nanny goat and her kid. From that link the children have been invited to

a local foundry to watch hot metal being worked from the viewing room and are already preparing for their 'Transport' topic by
making moulds themselves, starting with moulds of their hands.
As the company's representative said, 'If you can get nursery
children to understand what we do you might explain it to my
board'.

Conclusion

Obviously, before I collected this information, having known
Parkway Nursery over several years, I was aware of a number of
initiatives that had taken place there. I could not know, however,
the detail in the planning and co-ordination at all stages, and the
web of relationships that supports this. These are evident from
this description. Here is the evidence as to why partnership is important for this school. However, let us finish this section with
Mrs Andrews' own words:

> It's for the pupils, we're here for the pupils. At the end of the
> day it's the children that count. By having this method the
> pupils get a better education and each individual is catered
> for within the school, within the community. I will know
> where to get childminders for parents. I will know which
> agency we draw on. I will know who to go to from my links
> with the community and the under-fives group. I will know
> where they can get extra help.

ASHLEY COMMUNITY SCHOOL

Now as a comparison, I want to introduce the nursery class at
Ashley School. As will be seen, many of the responses to partnership at Ashley are very similar, but there are different emphases.
Some of these stem from the quite different circumstances of a
nursery class in a large school. Thus, this class is much smaller
than Parkway Nursery; it is part of a larger unit; the teacher in
charge works within a larger hierarchy; it exists within a different
community. All of these features bring with them different issues.

Ashley Community School is a large (420 on roll) Victorian
primary school in an old suburb of a large city. It is surrounded
by neat, newly refurbished terrace housing and some newly built
'starter homes'. Eighty-five per cent of the children's families are

South Asian in origin, mainly having Mirpuri Punjabi and Sylheti Bengali as their first language. Some children speak Vietnamese and Malay; 5 per cent of the children are white.

Within the last few years the whole school has been extensively refurbished, and at this point a thirty-nine place nursery was added, employing one teacher in charge (Mrs Manson) and two nursery nurses. It is situated at the end of the school, next to the reception class and has one large open plan classroom, a small withdrawal room and staffroom. As its name suggests, Ashley School tries to promote teamwork and a sense of community within the school in several ways. 'As a community school we want to see parents around the school.'

Planning

Thus, as Mrs Manson acknowledged, to ensure coherence, planning in this nursery, although similar to that at Parkway, takes place within the context of the whole school, from Year 6 to nursery, and within the school's development plan, the basic framework of which is worked out by the senior management team. The whole staff decided to work to issue-based topics which would lend themselves to a cross-curricular approach and these were allocated termly to each year band. In the autumn the nursery's topic is 'Me and My Family', in spring, 'People Who Help Us', and in the summer the whole school explores different aspects of 'Relationships'. The nursery, in particular, aims to use the topics to develop children's self-esteem and sense of importance, incorporate aspects of their culture and include some of the festivals that occur, especially in the autumn term.

Although Mrs Manson has oversight, detailed planning then takes place with the two nursery nurses, Carol Sims and Rukhsana Khan, so that, as with Parkway, the topic is matched with the development of skills and experiences. Each person takes responsibility for working on a different skill during a three week cycle. Thus, one person may be in charge of cutting and sticking, one puzzles, one printing. At the end of the three weeks all of the children have had experience of all three areas, again like Parkway ensuring coherence and consistency for them. Each week a different member of the team takes the lead in planning activities around these skills, but all benefit from 'bouncing ideas around' together.

Each member of staff has a 'family group' of children she is particularly responsible for, but, because of the room's small area, the children learn to relate to all the adults working there and only separate for the convenience of grouping for story or going out to play. Much of the work is one to one and, ideally, matched to the development of the child. 'There can be a vast difference between a child who is just three and someone who is nearly four. It's like a university degree if you like.'

Underlying this pattern of working are stated aims of this school: access and entitlement. As Mrs Manson put it:

> You've got to have some kind of partnership. There's no way you're going to deliver the curriculum to seventy odd children and ensure that they've all got equal access. So you've got to have a way of devolving the power, keeping control over the way it's delivered and entitlement in as much as each child, whether they've got a morning place or an afternoon place, gets as far as possible equal access.

Again, it is clear that work is very much shared and in such a small working area communication and relationships are important. Interestingly, Mrs Manson talked in a similar way to Mrs Andrews about the difference in roles.

> The difference is in terms of responsibility. I am aware that I am the one who takes the flak. If a parent is going to be stroppy I say 'that's me, I'll deal with it'. I defend staff at the end of the day. If they've done something wrong then I'm responsible. That's how the head perceives it.

Similarly, she accepts extra commitments:

> I don't insist that they stay on after school. I don't insist that they work their lunch hours. I deal with all the agencies that phone up. I attend the meetings and inform them of what's going on, and I think it's working because they often say, 'I wouldn't want your job'. So they can see I do over and above what they're asked to do, but it's a never ending problem. A confusion over roles has developed. At one time a nursery nurse was here to make the tea and clean up the sick. Well that's long gone. There are advantages and disadvantages on both sides really.

At the same time, of course, transfer and communication is

helped because the nursery is so close to the reception classes. The children are being taught according to a similar philosophy, they have got over their fears of the school, movement is just across the playground to teachers they have seen many times before. Thankfully, for everyone's sake, the days of having half the reception class crying on the first day have gone.

Parents

How then had relationships with parents developed? As a new nursery it had a good start. It was well resourced and was able to respond to pressure in the area for nursery places, starting with children from the school's parents and toddlers group, without needing to canvass for customers. At first, however, unlike the rest of the school, there were few Asian children, so an early objective had been to make parents aware that there was a nursery and then to build up relationships so that they trusted the staff to have their children from a young age. This happened in a number of ways. Mrs Manson had taught previously in the infant department, knew children and families in the main school and made sure she was still a familiar face around the building. Priority was given to children with older brothers and sisters in the school who, it was felt, would stay, rather than take advantage of the nursery place and then move to another primary school. Then, gradually, older children who had been in the nursery would come to ask if their little brothers and sisters were on the list; mothers would pop in, bringing their next door neighbours.

The other strategy was to undermine what were felt to be received views about early years education. Staff noticed that in the younger classes attendance was much more casual but firmed up as the children reached Year 6, suggesting that education was seen as more important at this stage. This, then, has become an issue for the whole school to tackle in various ways.

Informally, nursery staff have a policy of button holing parents, showing them children's work, getting out the large assessment files and recording sheets and indicating children's progress, 'do you know he can recognise his name in English?'. At the beginning of the year the staff take advantage of their 'captive audience' in the initial induction period, when parents stay with their children until they are settled, by running on the spot workshops. So, writing materials might be put out and as the children start what appears to be scribbling, staff talk to parents about early writing. 'We need to inform the parents about the importance of what we do, which is not always explicit. Why do children cut up magazines, for instance? You talk about developing co-ordination but take the jargon out.' This is a pattern in the rest of the school. Parents are encouraged to stay behind after dropping their children to attend parents' workshops started by the community education co-ordinator, which usually have a curriculum focus and where parents can try out materials. Arriving to talk to the teacher who was running one of these, within seconds I found myself manipulating the play dough thrust into my hand by Barbara, the enthusiastic classroom assistant.

Similarly, at nursery induction parents are involved in the initial 'baseline' assessment in discussing areas where they have been involved in teaching their child, perhaps to put on their coat, recognise their colours, or in reading stories together. 'We want to emphasise you're the first educator; you've taught them to do that. It's a feeling of a parent being involved in that process and the importance of that process.' Links between the parents themselves are also encouraged, so that the doors are opened in the morning for parents to come in with their children, but the staff stay in their meeting until 9 o'clock. 'It means they have to talk to each other and have to play with their children.' New parents get to know the others, and staff notice that by the middle of the school year a group is usually settled in the corner chatting until 9.30.

This in turn has meant that there are no problems in finding interpreters, 'other parents are ready to dive in, or they'll say, "oh actually she wants to know if he can stay for school dinners next week"'. Having parents who are relaxed and confident enough to interject had helped relationships all round, even though the school had built up a network of excellent, reliable interpreters, sign and letter writers and Mrs Khan, the nursery nurse, can speak Urdu and some Bengali.

Agencies

Like Mrs Andrews, Mrs Manson is a link to social services, health visitors, dentist, speech therapist, oral clinic and school nurse, often because these professionals are supporting a family under stress in its application for a place. Also like Mrs Andrews, she experiences frustration over feedback, particularly in locating the health visitor who knows a particular family, in getting appointments for certain conditions, such as hearing loss, and actually knowing whether the appointment has been kept. This problem of communication between agencies and the need for training in inter-agency collaboration has been noted in recent reports (Department of Health, 1995). Some contacts had been created in that the pre-school worker had been able to attend the local clinic, and was visiting three families to play with children over whom there had been concern. But, for the school 'there is a concern that we're not all working in the same direction' because of the different regulations for under-fives. Once the provision is statutory it was felt that the information flow improves.

A further strategy is that as part of the 'People Who Help Us' topic in the second term the dentist, the chiropodist, and the health visitor are invited in to give a presentation in the morning when parents have arrived and are a captive audience.

Conclusion

Here, then, is a nursery which is very much affected by the context of the school of which it is part. As with Parkway, I want to finish with Mrs Manson's view of what partnership means to her and why she values it.

> There are a lot of responsibilities I would like to hand back to parents which I can't at the moment because they don't see my role in the same light as myself. There are mixed messages about early years teaching which go across cultural boundaries in as much that the older the child you teach the more status you have. I'm totally aware that is one of the fundamental things I will always have to fight in this context. Therefore, I am a day carer not a teacher. I feel that the policies that are engendered by the government and the local authority, which is get more women back into work for low paid jobs, that just sends the message 'day care', it doesn't send the message if your child gets into a nursery at three they are far more likely to succeed. I am down here trying to get the message across, this is about education not baby sitting. The image of nursery education really concerns me, the potential of its provision.

AND FINALLY...

Many aspects of partnership and what it means for these two schools will have become clear during the description, and I will now note some of them.

- The concept of partnership has wide application and incorporates the 'culture of collaboration' within the school, noted by Nias (1989), and the web of relationships made with the outside world.
- It is a visible commitment by the school. Policy does not remain as declarations in documents but is put into action.
- It creates a momentum of its own. Every opportunity is made to take advantage of initiatives and build up networks and relationships of all kinds.
- Key personnel work from a clear conceptual base and are articulate about their practice. They are pro-active and innovative.
- There is an acceptance that all of those involved can learn from each other and that each contribution will be valued, whatever an individual's status or relationship might be. Interdependence is accepted as a norm, each person is 'a peece of the Continent, a part of the maine'.
- It is supported by open systems of communication, clear role definitions, a shared philosophy, and sustained by a recognition that personal relationships are as important as the routines of work.

REFERENCES

Abbott, R., Birchenough, M. and Steadman, S. (1988) *Guidelines for Review and Internal Development in Schools*, London: Schools Curriculum Development Committee.

Biott, C. and Easen, P. (1994) *Collaborative Learning in Staffrooms and Classrooms*, London: Fulton.

David, T. (ed.) (1994) *Working Together for Young Children*, London: Routledge.

Department of Health and OFSTED (1995) *The Education of Children Who are Looked After by Local Authorities*, London: HMSO.

Nias, J. (1989) *Primary Teachers Talking: A study of teaching as work*, London: Routledge.

APPENDIX 1: PARKWAY NURSERY DAY PLAN

	Water	Construction	Easel	Writing table	Carpet	Computer
N1 Wednesday a.m.	*Green* Carole: Marbling	√ Jane: Collage robots	√	√*Felts* Geraldine: Soup tasting	√*Big bricks*	
N2 Wednesday a.m.	Role play *Opticians* Mary: Cooking biscuits	Adele: Cutting circles	Jigsaws	Role play *Tunnel*		Kathy: Floating and sinking
N3 Wednesday a.m.	*Blue toys clear water*	Sand *Wet*	Easel *Yellow paper*	Role play *Home & babies*	Big bricks	Old Mac
N1 Wednesday p.m.	*Green* Carole: Records, pencil skills	√ Jane: Clay	√	√*Birds* Geraldine: Graph about soup tasting		
N2 Wednesday p.m.	Role play *Opticians* Jane: Scissor skills Lotto cards		Jigsaws Kathy: Language (farm)	Role play *Tunnel*		Mary: painting papier mâché balloons
N3 Wednesday p.m.	√ Adele: Table top painting of animals	Sand √	√	Role play √ Ann: Farm animals & mat	*Animal puppets*	Old Mac

APPENDIX 2: PARKWAY NURSERY RECORD SHEET

Name:

Language

Can ask for help: using gestures   using language

Speech is easily understood by others

Follows simple instructions: one to one   small group   large group

Responds to conversation with staff: using phrases   whole statements   group talk

Responds to conversation with children: using phrases   whole statements   group talk

Relationships

Attitude to staff: friendly   shy   avoids

Staff attention: constantly seeks   enjoys   avoids

Seeks affection with staff: constantly seeks   enjoys   avoids

Attitude to peers: friendly   shy   avoids

Play patterns

Solitary play: own choice   excluded

Group play: initiates   follows

Co-operative play: shares and takes turns   forms consistent friendships

Copes with: frustration   conflict   distress   anger

Recovers equanimity in reasonable time

Colours
Matches
Names

Maths
Counts by rote
Counts objects
1-5 symbols Circle   Square   Triangle   Rectangle

2

PLANNING IN PARTNERSHIP
IN THE PRIMARY SCHOOL

Ann Lance and Anita Cliff

There was a time in the recent history of primary education when individual practitioners could lock themselves away in the confines of their own classrooms to carry out their roles as primary teachers. Similarly, they had a relatively free rein over the content of the curriculum, provided they complied with rather general schemes of work which the school management compiled. Thankfully the system became rather tighter during the 1980s and a whole school approach, both towards general organisation and policy, and the curriculum, became the norm. Postholders tended to be responsible for particular areas of the curriculum, and people were expected to work in phase or year group teams in the planning and delivery of the curriculum. The systems for planning varied from those which had a faculty approach and highly organised plans which took continuity and differentiation into account, to those which were less rigorous and sometimes resulted in children repeating topics year after year in their primary career.

And then along came the legislation of the late 1980s and early 1990s which brought a system which was much more ordered, which laid down quite clearly what should be taught, when it should be taught, and how it would be assessed. It arrived amidst a package of other radical changes in the primary system, not least the local financial management of schools, and, in many primary schools, the staff were thrown into a frenzy of inset and paper work which they found very difficult to cope with. The overkill in the curriculum during that period of the early 1990s led to a rush towards early retirement, a panic about the resourcing of subjects such as history and science in the early years, and a general feeling of lack of control in many schools.

Ultimately, there followed the slimmed down version of the National Curriculum, but, while many were very grateful to Sir Ron Dearing, this too brought its tensions. These comments from a primary headteacher bear this out:

Our planning initiative was damaged by the latest changes to the National Curriculum based on the Dearing Report. This means that much of the work already done had to be at least re-organised and in many cases scrapped altogether. This is a very demotivating situation for staff and it is by no means the first time it has happened.

However, in the post Dearing era, with a reduction in curriculum demand, where schools have learnt to adjust to the new mind-set of accountability, and they have begun to take advantage of their new found budgetary freedom, the dust has at last begun to settle.

It is in the wake of these developments that I want the reader to consider the concerns which primary teachers meet in planning in partnership in their schools. In the case study that follows you will have an opportunity to take a glimpse into one primary setting to view a variety of mechanisms for planning, and to reflect on a range of relevant issues.

However, before we look at this individual situation it is useful to examine some of the broader considerations which impinge on planning in primary schools in the 1990s. The reader can then compare and contrast this general overview with the individual case study which is presented.

CHANGE

The degree and nature of changes which have taken place over the past decade have meant that headteachers can no longer rely on the presence of a common whole school focus. Because of increased external accountability, both in terms of the curriculum and its assessment, and the expectations which have been built around the system of primary education, headteachers have been forced to employ a much more systematic approach to the development of planning within their school. They have also had to give considerable thought to the concept of change and its implications for both the individuals and the systems within their institutions. As one headteacher has observed:

For some time now I have felt that we are much better at reviewing, planning and monitoring initiatives for change in school, than we are at institutionalising the changes which we want to take place in the classroom. These changes are not only very difficult to measure but also very difficult to bring about and are often short-lived. So, in order for initiatives in the school to be effective, supported and sustained, I need to understand more about the nature of change itself.

There can be no doubt that change has a considerable impact on individual teachers. Michael Fullan (1993) reminds us that

> we have become so accustomed to change that we rarely stop to think what change really means as we are experiencing it at a personal level. More important, we almost never stop to think what it means for others around us who might be in change situation. The crux of change is how individuals come to grips with this reality.

Clearly, in the context of so many changes there is an urgent necessity to consider how they might be successfully managed.

Having raised awareness about this issue, Fullan (1993) goes on to identify three elements which need to be considered if change is to be made effectively.

- *The time factor*. It is highly unlikely that any change can be achieved over a short period of time. What he describes as 'quick-fix' solutions are rarely successful.
- *The weight of the school's current agenda*. Change will not be successfully brought about if it is introduced in a situation overload.
- *The available financial resources*. These need to be examined carefully before a major change is considered.

The third of these factors is exemplified by a statement made by a home school liaison teacher in relation to a planning initiative which she was leading:

> It would be foolish to believe that this scheme, like most others, was not dependent upon extra funding. What we have attempted to do is to look at alternative ways of achieving our aims should the funding not be available in the amounts we would hope for. However, the consensus of

opinion is that whatever the funding implications there is a need to look at this issue.

In the school case study that follows later, all three of these elements appear as significant issues.

Fullan develops his theme by describing the differing circumstances in which change may come about. Change occurs either because it is imposed on schools by natural events or deliberate reform, or because we voluntarily participate in or even initiate change when we find dissatisfaction with our current situation.

Again, in the case study, there is evidence that changes come about because of the external pressure of government driven reforms, but that these are often related to the participant practitioners' discontent with the planning systems which they are reviewing.

CREATING THE CLIMATE FOR CHANGE

One of the essential elements in introducing change in planning systems is that whoever the instigator of the change is, be it class teacher, curriculum leader or headteacher, they must allow the other parties involved to have time to come to terms with the proposed change. This point is well made by Marris (1975):

> Every attempt to pre-empt conflict, argument, protest by rational planning, can only be abortive; however reasonable the proposed changes, the process of implementing them must still allow the impulse of rejection to play itself out. When those who have power to manipulate changes act as if they have only to explain, and when their explanations are not at once accepted, shrug off opposition as ignorance or prejudice, they express a profound contempt for the meaning of lives other than their own. For the reformers have already assimilated these changes to their purposes, and worked out a reformulation which makes sense to them, perhaps through months or years of analysis and debate. If they deny others the chance to do the same, they treat them as puppets dangling by the threads of their own conception.

There is a real tension here because the person responsible for implementing a change in planning within a school runs the risk of leaving colleagues behind, or dragging them along screaming, if they do not allow time for them to 'grow into' the idea of a change. They could find themselves guilty of the same error which central government made by trying to introduce too much, too quickly, if they do not allow for this period of debate which Marris describes so well. On the other hand, for the instigator of the change, external pressures may well come into play which do not allow them the luxury of marking time in the hope that the rest of the team will follow suit. Again the case study illustrates this dilemma which both headteachers and curriculum leaders wrestle with.

In addition to allowing a period of time for others to be drawn along, planning leaders need to reflect on the reasons why teachers may be resistant. Fullan (1993) argues that teacher isolation may be an important factor here. Working in the same classroom day in and day out, may have the effect of:

- encouraging a short-term perspective;
- isolating them from other adults;
- exhausting their energy; and
- limiting their opportunities for sustained reflection.

There may be limitations on ways in which planning agents within a primary school can influence these factors, but it seems clear, as the previous chapter indicated, that it is essential to create the right climate and working conditions for teachers if they are to be encouraged to participate in change. Fullan reminds us that we must take into account that the development of a collaborative planning approach is even more challenging than ever because:

- the conditions of teaching appear to have deteriorated over the past two decades;
- teachers have become devalued by the community and public; and
- teacher stress and alienation from the profession are at an all time high.

It is important, therefore, that when embarking on an initiative which involves change planning leaders have an awareness of these issues and consider the starting point for their colleagues. This is not to say that they should excuse negative responses from colleagues, but rather that they should consider the pressures and alternative priorities which staff could be experiencing.

LEADERSHIP

Another major area of consideration in relation to collaborative planning in primary schools is that of leadership. Earlier models of leadership in primary schools placed great emphasis on the role of the headteacher. Effective leadership was often described in terms of qualities which were the sole domain of this person. While there is no doubt that the role of the headteacher is crucial in the running of a school, there has been some concern that concentrating on the personal and professional qualities of a single individual does not provide a comprehensive model for impact on practice in the primary school. Caldwell and Spinks (1989) argue that the study of leadership across a variety of multidisciplinary settings has led to the identification of two important aspects of this contemporary view of leadership. These are: (a) vision in leadership and (b) fostering of leadership.

Vision

Vision is an expression of a desirable direction and destination for a school underpinned by the school's own philosophy. It must engage with the history of the school, the development of its ethos, its successes and failures, previous strategies for improvement, and earlier attempts to articulate a way forward. . . . Most important, vision must look confidently towards the future: pointing the way forward for all those involved in the school.

(Anon., 1995)

It is clear from this definition that vision is not the sole responsibility of the headteacher. Indeed, vision imposed by a single individual is more likely to be resisted by those who will be required to implement it, and is more likely to decline after that individual leaves the school. A shared vision, on the other hand, is likely to impact positively on the planning process. This comment from a Key Stage 1 teacher illustrates one mechanism for developing vision in the planning process: 'Our vision had been formed by reviewing the situation we were in, and identifying our whole school strengths'. The potential impact which vision may have on those involved in collaborative planning within a school is threefold:

- it encourages them to re-evaluate the way in which they do things;
- it motivates them to make changes in line with a common ideal for the evolution of the school; and
- they are empowered, awarded greater status, and given confidence (Anon., 1995).

Fostering leadership

In the same way that vision is seen as a mechanism for collaborative school management, there is a need for the headteacher to be proactive in fostering leadership amongst all members of the staff team. It is apparent from the following comments, written by a primary teacher, that where headteachers see part of their role as extending the responsibilities and duties of leadership within the school, that participation and sharing of leadership follow.

> Staff at all levels were seen as managers, able to take decisions affecting their area of responsibility. This was mainly due to the philosophy of the headteacher.... Thus, staff were used to taking decisions and prompting action. This has led to a situation in the school where everyone has value as a manager and decision maker.

Caldwell and Spinks (1989) reinforce this notion of the importance of delegation: 'Collaborative School Management fosters many leaders in teams for programme planning and in working parties on policy-related issues.' It seems clear that planning in primary schools in the 1990s requires the active leadership of all staff members. The implications for headteachers of collaborative team management in planning the curriculum are that they must:

- have sufficient confidence in their individual team members to allow them to take responsibility for aspects of the curriculum;
- allow them time to carry out their role; and
- provide them with the resources to support initiatives.

This is not an exercise in mere delegation, but rather one which requires considerable development and support.

SUMMARY

Now that we have looked at these broad elements – change, climate and leadership – a number of specific questions emerge which will be considered in relation to the case study that follows and which will highlight significant aspects supporting planning in partnership.

* What mechanisms can staff employ to facilitate a collaborative approach to planning?
* What are the challenges of engaging in such a process?
* What are the benefits of planning in partnership?

A CASE STUDY OF PLANNING: REVISING A SCHOOL'S PROJECT CYCLE

The background

The curriculum co-ordinator led this innovation. At the school there was in place a cross-curricular project system which encompassed the whole of the science, technology, history, geography and music National Curriculum documents. RE themes permeated all the projects. With the introduction of new National Curriculum orders it was necessary to adjust the project cycle to satisfy post Dearing proposals. In addition, various members of staff played crucial roles. The suggestion for embarking on this change came from a new member when colleagues were discussing the implications of the new National Curriculum. Staff appeared keen to update the projects and use the demands of the new documentation as an opportunity to develop their projects. The current project cycle had been in place for two years and, as a result of teaching for that length of time, staff had clear ideas of how to develop them.

From this initial discussion there was obviously still a firm commitment and belief in the project approach. The staff said they felt it provided children with a context for their learning and that it created an environment in which the children could succeed. The curriculum co-ordinator was responsible for developing these projects and she saw this as an ideal opportunity to begin restructuring them with the support of the staff from a very positive starting point. She felt that the initiative had come from the staff, and that their fundamental concern to develop the projects would ensure some success. She was pleased that, in contrast to a whole range of imposed initiatives since 1988, for this initiative they would be starting from a common whole school focus, which she felt sure would generate interest and enthusiasm.

However, it was clear that the project document which they were seeking to amend was a very comprehensive one and updating and developing it would require a considerable amount of time and effort. Each project had been assigned appropriate attainment targets and programmes of study which were to be covered for each of the subjects noted previously. Each subject section had been documented with ideas and starting points which could deliver the specified attainments and programmes of study. The projects built on experiences and attainment targets in a spiral manner to ensure that each level of the National Curriculum was covered thoroughly and built upon progressively. The starting point for this change was to build upon past achievements, evaluating the present situation and looking for ways to move forward.

Development

To gather the views of all staff on the existing project document and gather ideas about its future development, the curriculum co-ordinator gave out a questionnaire (Appendix 1). Because of the need to match the new projects to the new National Curriculum orders the questions were framed in relation to this. They asked individuals what they thought their contribution could be towards the new project cycle, as well as asking each member of staff about the format the new document should take and their estimate of the time scale required to re-create such a comprehensive document. The response to the questionnaire was very positive on the whole, with each staff member completing it and returning it within two days. One of the most significant factors which emerged from the questionnaires was the time factor. Staff felt that with just over half a term to go until the end of the school year it would be impossible to complete such an initiative. Several members of staff said that although they thought the project was an important and necessary one, they felt it was the wrong time of the year to attempt to start it, and that it would be more appropriate to do so at the beginning of the new school year. At the same time, the majority of staff were happy to commit themselves to a curriculum area even where they had no specific responsibility to do so, and most postholders seemed happy to work on their curriculum areas with others on the project themes, taking into account the new National Curriculum.

At this point the co-ordinator began to worry that while the initiative was relevant and that people were obviously ready for the change, resourcing, particularly in terms of time, was not available. Because of this pressure some staff began to express doubt about the future of the initiative. What could be done? The curriculum co-ordinator decided to talk to staff individually to 'tackle their concerns and discuss the way forward in more detail'. In this way she hoped to be able to take into account each member's concerns and build upon their enthusiasms. Her intention at this point was to suggest a model of incremental change and tackle one curriculum area at a time. She therefore set up times for meetings with all postholders and designed a discussion document to guide the interview (Appendix 2).

Postholder meetings

In the first of these interviews the member of staff revealed that, while she agreed with the idea of reviewing the project cycle and wanted to be involved, she felt that the timing of the present initiative was wrong. She had some very innovative ideas but felt that she did not have time to put them into action. In response the curriculum co-ordinator offered her the support of two staff members and word-processing assistance, and as a result of this offer she agreed to try to meet the deadline. The rest of the meetings followed much the same pattern with staff agreeing to spend as much time as they could on contributing sections to the document.

The co-ordinator was much encouraged by the fact that four members of staff who were not curriculum postholders said that they were very pleased to be involved, and had not felt this to be the case before. This served as a reminder that the demands over past years had led to less corporate involvement and more top-down direction.

The whole school approach, which staff repeatedly reminded me was once a part of the school's fabric, had regenerated. The staff were really enthusiastic about the project because it was involving everyone in some way. A common response from these individual meetings was the expression of pride in the original document and an affirmation of its usefulness as a tool for planning in the classroom. One member of staff said, 'to work upon what we have already achieved is quite an exciting prospect. It's really good to build upon a success instead of starting from scratch, or from a criticism about something we are not doing properly!' Another commented, 'This approach should ensure success as very often things are imposed upon class teachers, they have no input.'

The co-ordinator proceeded to group people into subject areas so that each postholder had someone working with them to share the workload. At this stage she met the headteacher and requested that he might cancel all staff meetings during the following weeks so that they could be rescheduled for project meetings. He not only agreed to this but also offered to join one of the groups to offer his support. At this point she began to feel very positive once again as it meant that everyone was involved. She offered to word process all the constituent parts but was very pleased to have an offer of help from a colleague, particularly as the original document had been fifty pages long!

Staff meeting

The whole staff meeting was held in order to clarify working groups and their brief, and to thank people for their commitment towards the project. It was also felt to be important that staff should meet and be aware of the whole picture and how the project worked as a shared venture. 'I felt it would give everyone a sense of community, and would enhance staff collaboration.'

Staff looked closely at the project themes for Reception, Key Stage 1 and Key Stage 2 and alterations were made to fit the new National Curriculum guidelines (Appendix 3). There followed discussion about how the document would be set out and what would be included in it. This discussion was lively and an agreement was made that as much as possible would be completed by the end of term. The group agreed to adopt the style of the former project document, to include curriculum programmes of study for each subject, and activities and starting points to deliver these. It was also agreed that year group teachers should be satisfied with the project content before it was accepted as part of the new document. Staff felt that, given that the National Curriculum was not going to change during the coming five years, this should be a document which they could be satisfied with and which would stand the test of that period of time. It was acknowledged that some curriculum areas, such as science, would take longer to complete than others, and that if some staff completed their section they would offer their services to another working group. This meant that the whole document could be completed in an incremental fashion, as the curriculum co-ordinator had anticipated. It was generally agreed that, when project plans for curriculum areas were completed in draft form, postholders should get in touch with curriculum advisers and contacts in the field of higher education with whom the school had links to ask for their input. One member of staff commented, 'If we are going to do them we might as well do them properly. With specialist input as well as our own work we could really develop what we have already!'

Consultation

Over the following weeks groups of people began to work on the project sections with advisory teachers for history and information technology being invited into school. The science group visited a local university and asked for support from science and technology staff who had worked closely with the school in the past. It was apparent that many meetings and discussions were going on before school, at lunchtime and after school. Staff would stop the curriculum co-ordinator in the corridor to show her sections they had started, and tell her of ideas they had begun to develop. The whole school seemed busy with project planning.

The venture was not without its pressures as far as the co-ordinator was concerned.

At times, if I was perfectly honest, I felt quite pressurised as pieces of paper were being handed to me to be word processed in piles and piles. Even with some help getting this it was taking up an enormous amount of time. I felt as if I should get it done as it was given to me. I did not want to hold up this terrific momentum of enthusiasm.

Review and evaluation

By the end of the term the project document was not completed, but significant inroads had been made in moving towards it. The science section had been agreed by each year group in the school. It had also been developed with the support of the teaching staff at the university, and was finished. The history, geography, technology and information technology sections were complete in note form, had been agreed by all year groups and developed with the support from advisory teachers. Religious education, music, art, creative language and mathematics were nearly completed also, awaiting year group meetings to approve them. Given three or four more weeks the document would have been ready for the new school year.

A brief staff meeting was called by the curriculum co-ordinator during the last week to show everyone what had been achieved so far. Staff were impressed and there was general commitment to complete the document in the new school year. The co-ordinator summed up her feelings about the initiative in the following way:

> The initiative has allowed all staff to become involved and, therefore, given them ownership of the development. Staff have been given the chance to collaborate, to draw upon the specialist expertise of each other and of outside agencies and produce something they will find purposeful.
>
> The intention is that the momentum will be sustained and that the document will be completed in the following term. I feel we have experienced success, a success I am convinced we are all looking forward to building upon in the new school year. It is clear that the process of this planning in partnership has been as fruitful as the outcome in terms of documentation will be in the future.

CONCLUSION

What have we learnt about working in partnership to manage change? I feel that the following elements must be considered:

- First, change is a very complex phenomenon and has unforeseen consequences.

45

- Changes often come about as a result of external pressure driven by internal need.
- If change is to be managed effectively, the resource implications must be reviewed. In particular, overloading colleagues should be avoided or alleviated.
- A period of time must be allowed for all the participants in change to have the opportunity to debate the issue.
- The climate for collaboration in a particular school must be taken into account, especially how to incorporate or develop a shared vision in planning.
- Collaborative school management and the fostering of leadership at all levels are essential to the planning process.

REFERENCES

Anon. (1995) *Research Matters, The School Improvement Network Bulletin,* Institute of Education, University of London.

Caldwell, B.J. and Spinks, J.M. (1989) *Leading the Self-Managing School,* London: Falmer.

Fullan, M. (1993) *The New Meaning of Educational Change,* London: Cassell.

Marris, P. (1975) *Loss and Change,* New York: Anchor Press.

APPENDIX 1: STAFF PROJECT QUESTIONNAIRE

1 What do you think about our current project document?
2 How often do you use it?
3 Do you think it would be useful to update and develop it to match new National Curriculum orders and staff development ideas?
4 How best do you think you could be involved in such a project?
5 If you are not responsible for a curriculum area, which area would you feel happiest working in?
6 Do you think it would be possible to start such a project this term?
7 How long do you think such a project would take to complete?

APPENDIX 2: STRUCTURED DISCUSSION DOCUMENT FOR INDIVIDUAL STAFF

- What aspects of projects do we need to look at?
  – Identification of development needs:
- Where are we now?
  – Stocktaking, from individual perspective, gathering of evidence of present situation.
- Where do we want to be?
  – Target setting.
- How can we get there?
  – Strategic planning.
- Individual input. What could it be?
- Time?

APPENDIX 3: PROJECT CYCLE

Year	Autumn term	Spring term	Summer term
R	Letterland	Stories and Numbers	Nursery Rhymes
1	Journeys	All About Me and What I Eat	Splash
2	Changes	Flash, Crash, Rumble & Roll	Protection
3	Me and Other Things that Grow/Me & My Clothes (HU – Local History – School grounds/where we live)	A Cup of Tea/Food (HU – Farming)	Ancient Greece/On The Move (HU – Ancient Greece)
4	Protection/Invaders (HU – Invaders/ settlers)	Communication/ Space (HU – Transport)	Our Neighbourhood/ Travel & Tourism (HU – Local History Lozells)
5	Structures/Bodies & Bones (HU – Tudors & Stuarts)	Journeys/Flight (HU – Local History 2nd World War)	Storms/Our City (HU – Local History – Birmingham)
6	Our World/Light & Colour (HU – Aztecs/Exploration & Encounters)	The 20th Century/Machines & Industry (HU – Britain Since the 1930s)	Ancient Egypt/Beneath the Surface (HU – Ancient Egypt

HU = History study unit.

3

SUPPORTING PUPILS WITH SPECIAL EDUCATIONAL NEEDS

Penny Lacey

One of the areas in which teachers are undoubtedly in partnership with other people is working with pupils with special educational needs (SEN). Although some SEN will be fleeting and the curriculum and teaching can be adjusted to accommodate specific pupils, others will be more complex and will involve the expertise of several different people. Bringing this together so that it all works smoothly is taxing and a task which needs considerable management skills. In this chapter I will discuss some of the problems and possibilities and give advice concerning the ways in which you, the teacher, can organise yourself and the other adults who will be working with you in your classroom.

First, it will be helpful briefly to consider special educational needs in general so that you can see the management task in context. The way in which special educational needs are tackled in the 1990s emanates very largely from the Warnock Report (DES, 1978) and the ensuing Education Act 1981, although what is contained in this act has become Section III of the 1993 Education Act. The nature of SEN is very loosely defined and covers any pupil who has a need which is different from that of the majority. The Warnock Report suggested that as many as one in five children will, at some time in their school career, have a special need, indicating that the vast majority of teachers will be expected to teach pupils who have needs over and above the norm.

A central recommendation of the Warnock Report was that pupils with SEN should be educated in ordinary schools where possible. There was a recognition, however, that some pupils would be better served in special schools and units, especially those with more severe and complex difficulties. This was a departure from previous ways of managing special needs, when it

48

was expected that pupils displaying difficulties would automatically be transferred to a special environment. Since the beginning of the 1980s this shift has meant an enormous growth in the number and range of personnel engaged in meeting the needs of the wide variety of pupils in mainstream schools.

There has also been a growth of certain staff in special schools and units as the character of these has changed over the last twenty years. Since the 1970 Education (Handicapped Children) Act, pupils with severe and profound learning difficulties have been included in education. Until this time, they were deemed 'ineducable' and were placed in training centres run by the Health Service. Bringing these pupils into education was the spur for appointing a wealth of ancillary staff to work alongside teachers in the classroom. Help was needed with care tasks such as toileting and dressing and often 'another pair of hands' was essential when dealing with pupils with very difficult behaviour.

With the improvement of medical science, more children with complex difficulties are surviving birth and infancy and are being educated in schools. They present teachers with an enormous number of problems which are beyond the scope of one person. No longer is it possible for teachers to work alone in education. Whether in mainstream or special schools, teachers need other people to work with them, to support them and to advise them. Ancillaries have already been mentioned and they are part of the answer to this need for help for classroom teachers but there are many others such as Local Education Authority (LEA) support services and personnel from other agencies such as health and social services. The RNIB surveyed a group of forty-seven pupils with multiple disabilities to find out how many professionals were involved in their care and education (RNIB, 1992). They found a staggering twenty-seven.

Most children will not have a network of professionals quite as large as that but there will often be several people whose job it is to support pupils and their families through their school years. A child with physical disabilities might have a physiotherapist, a speech therapist, an occupational therapist, a nurse, and a welfare assistant as well as teachers all concerned with day-to-day care and education. There may also be a role for the support services if there is a pronounced learning difficulty or sensory impairment. Clearly there is a strong need for this to be managed in a way that it really is a help rather than a hindrance.

THE CODE OF PRACTICE

The Code of Practice on the Identification and Assessment of Special Educational Needs (DFE, 1994) contains advice for teachers and sets out the management task for meeting needs. The role of the special educational needs co-ordinator (SENCO) is also explicated. This is a key person in terms of help and support in mainstream schools. SENCOs are usually senior members of staff who are responsible for co-ordinating everything pertaining to SEN. They should have a register of all pupils with SEN and a list of different services for teachers to consult. They should also organise liaison with other agencies and generally be responsible for managing the school's response to the learning needs of pupils with difficulties.

Under the legislation, some pupils with SEN will have Statements of Special Educational Needs. These are the result of a comprehensive assessment by several different professionals. The Educational Psychologist usually co-ordinates this and the resulting statement will contain the basics of the provision and services that should be available for individual pupils. When you have a child with SEN in your class this is where you should begin to look for support in meeting these needs. The SENCO will have access to statements and will help you to understand their implications. They are important documents and should contain advice on the resources needed for carrying out the individual educational plan. These statements are reviewed annually so that changing needs and progress can be monitored.

There will be many other pupils with SEN whose needs are not considered severe enough for the protection of a statement. These may be relatively short term but they may also need extra resources in terms of staff. Schools in economically deprived areas may have a significant number of pupils who fall into this category and the presence of welfare personnel may be vital for enabling the children to take advantage of the education on offer. Representatives from the learning support services may also be much in evidence.

WORKING IN TEAMS

That brief summary of some of the aspects of SEN has given a picture of potential chaos. Personnel from a variety of different services could be involved with pupils in your class. Each child with SEN could have a different set of people supporting them. Although a learning support teacher may have several children from one class on his or her books, social workers tend to take on whole families and these rarely match up with schools and classes. Sometimes these personnel know each other well and have worked together for several different children but others will not even know of each other's existence. It is often the class teacher who has the job of bringing them all together for the individual pupils in their classes.

The term 'teamwork' is used to describe what happens to meet the needs of pupils with SEN. For some disabilities this should be multi-disciplinary in that representatives of several disciplines (education, health and social services) will be working together. There are, unfortunately, many times when teamwork is not really achieved. Members of these so-called teams hardly ever meet, do not plan or work together and on occasions even fight over territory they believe is being encroached. Teamwork may be a very worthy goal but it is very hard to achieve. The rest of this chapter is concerned with the difficulties experienced by school personnel attempting to work in teams and ideas for making this a reality.

Teamwork is essential if SEN are to be met in an efficient and effective manner. Consider this example:

The educational psychologist enters the classroom saying that she has been asked to observe John Smith who appears to have language and behaviour difficulties. She spends ten minutes in general observation and then withdraws the child to carry out a test. She returns John saying that she has administered a test of comprehension and expression and will send in the report in next week.

Two days later, the speech therapist arrives and also withdraws John. She returns him to say that she has administered a test of comprehension and expression and when her report comes in, it is obviously the same test as the educational psychologist used.

Clearly there is no evidence of co-ordination, in fact there has been little communication between the different agencies. Time and scarce resources have been wasted and multi-disciplinary teamwork has been demonstrated to be expensive.

In the face of such an example it is hard to persuade managers and policy-makers that teamwork is affordable, but when it works well and after the initial pump priming, it can be seen to be cost effective and likely to meet a variety of needs.

TEAMS AND NETWORKS

The definitions of different partnership arrangements which follow refer to SEN, but echo the features of teams, networks and collaborative working relationships which are described in other chapters. As far as meeting SEN goes it can be helpful to view working together on a continuum (Lacey, 1995). It is not possible to have the same level of teamwork with everyone. There are too many people involved to make that viable. First it is useful to differentiate between a team and a network.

A team is a group in which the individuals have a common aim and in which the jobs and skills of each member fit in with those of others, as . . . in a jigsaw puzzle pieces fit together without distortion and together produce an overall pattern.

(Babington-Smith and Farrell, 1979)

This is a very close working relationship where individuals see each other on a daily basis and their work is deliberately inter-related. Teachers and classroom assistants can have this kind of working relationship. In special schools, this tight-knit team may extend to therapists and in residential schools to residential social workers but it basically refers to a small number of people who are in day-to-day contact with the child. It is desirable to include parents in this inner team. Chapters 4 and 5 describe other ways of working in partnership with parents on literacy skills.

A network, on the other hand, contains a much broader set of people (Payne, 1993), as Mary Comber indicates in Chapter 6. These may be involved with meeting SEN in your classroom infrequently or perhaps just once for a specific pupil. They are, however, a resource and part of the rich variety of personnel on whom you can call. There is no way you can have a close team-like relationship with all these people but you do need to know who they are, what they can offer and how to get in touch with them when you need them.

Within the network, you will be expected to *liaise* with different services and staff. This refers to the minimum contact necessary for enabling the network to function. Knowing each other's roles, expertise, resources and availability are essential to liaison. With some members you will be expected to *co-operate*. This refers to ensuring that you and the various support services know what each other are doing and do not stand in each other's way. With others you will be expected to *co-ordinate* the work. This involves making sure that two people do not carry out the same assessment or arrive to see pupils at the same time and that reports from different sources are drawn together to make sense for you and for your pupils.

With your classroom team, you will be expected to *collaborate*. This implies all of the duties outlined above plus a togetherness which is impossible to achieve with staff who visit your classroom infrequently. Collaboration involves a willingness on the part of individuals to share expertise, plan jointly, work alongside each other, exchange roles and support each other completely. It is partnership born from a desire to meet SEN in an integrated manner and in the realisation that no one person can do this alone (Lacey and Lomas, 1993).

CLASSROOM ASSISTANTS

Although there may be other personnel in the classroom team, for the rest of this chapter I shall address the relationship which exists between teachers and classroom assistants. Most of the points I make could equally apply to working with other team members such as therapists, social workers and support teachers. I have chosen to concentrate on assistants as there are an increasing number of these staff in special and mainstream schools and there is very little written about the most effective way in which they can be part of the school and class teams.

There are many different terms used to describe assistants: welfare assistant, special support assistant, auxiliary, non-teaching assistant, teacher's aide and nursery nurse are but a few. Only nursery nurses, as a professional group, hold a recognised training and many people start their lives as classroom assistants with no training of any kind (Balshaw, 1991b; Clough and Lindsay, 1991). I have, however, heard of untrained assistants referred to as nursery nurses when in fact they do not hold the required certificate. This can be a source of difficulties, especially if there are both trained and untrained personnel on one staff. For the purposes of this chapter I am going to use the term 'assistants' whether or not these people are trained. This is not because I feel that training is not important but because it is an umbrella term which seems to encapsulate the role very well. This person is in the classroom to give assistance to the teacher and to the pupils.

Deciding on the role for an assistant is a very good place to start. It should be part of an exercise to define the roles of everyone working in the classroom. Balshaw's research (1991a) suggested that assistants are able to work more effectively when they have a clear idea of their roles. This is so even in a collaborative team where team members will be expected to fulfil parts of other people's roles. For instance:

> Mrs Jones (teacher) has been on a course about micro-computers and special needs. She has passed on the information to Mrs Brown (assistant). Now they are both able to work with the pupils. Anyone watching a microcomputer session supervised by either would not be able to distinguish between the two people.

There is no suggestion that all aspects of the job will be so indistinguishable but that some parts will be within the capabilities of both people. This might be so if it concerns basic positioning for pupils with physical disabilities or medical help for pupils with diabetes or asthma. It will be so for expectations of behaviour, amounts of independence and how to form letter shapes. Everyone who is in close proximity with pupils must agree on these basics so that they receive a consistent approach.

It is not enough for teachers to work out what they want and tell their assistants. If the team is to be really collaborative, this must be done together. All the research that has been carried out on managing change in organisations such as schools, points to the need for everyone who will be affected by that change to be involved in its inception (Fullan, 1993). People do not respond well when they are told what to do, especially if they do not understand why they are being asked to change from what they were doing. They are much more likely to co-operate and put policy into practice if they have been directly involved in devising it.

While the overlapping parts of roles are being discussed and developed, it is necessary to be clear about the specialist aspects of the teacher and assistant. It may be that the assistant has been engaged to meet the needs of one specific pupil. The child's statement of SEN will make clear what this should entail though there is bound to be room for interpretation.

Mrs Sand was appointed as a special support assistant for Ann who has been assessed as having autism. Ann has many temper tantrums and can be very disruptive to the rest of the class. As one of her duties, Mrs Sand removes Ann from the situation she is finding frustrating so that she can calm down and so that the rest of the class can continue.

As part of her role, this assistant has had to develop the specialist ability to get to know one pupil's needs in great detail. She is seen as the expert in this particular aspect of classroom life. It is likely that the teacher will have some of the skills of the assistant but her expertise lies in enabling that individual child to learn to the best of her abilities.

This can be taken too far. Consider this next example:

Mrs Todd is an assistant in a class of children of 'all abilities'. There are twenty children, three of whom have statements of SEN. They are described as having learning difficulties that are either moderate or severe in nature. Mrs Todd spends the large majority of her time with these three pupils who sit in a group in the middle of the classroom. She is a very capable member of staff who works well with this group. The teacher, Miss Ward, discusses the children's needs with Mrs Todd but only very rarely does she teach them. Most of the time they work away at their own level in an isolated group. When there is a whole class lesson perhaps on history or geography, which is beyond the comprehension level of this little group, they continue to work on their own on basic reading and writing skills or go outside to play a game.

Apart from the fact that this is very dubious integration, it is obvious that these three pupils see very little of their teacher. Although Mrs Todd is a very competent person and is trusted to work with these pupils, her role and that of the teacher have been defined in a way which appears to preclude overlap and flexibility. Results of a survey reported by MacConville (1991) indicated that the more complex the children's needs, the higher the level of non-teaching support and in consequence the less direct support from a qualified teacher. It is important to get the balance right.

Another aspect of defining roles that can present problems is that pertaining to status. Teachers have spent four years in training and command a salary considerably larger than that of assistants. I have worked in schools where this has been a serious barrier to harmonious working. In one, assistants complained that they were expected to do the work of a teacher for a fraction of the pay. They resented being expected to perform a teaching role, feeling that they were neither trained nor financially rewarded for so doing. Consider though an example from another school:

> When Mrs Davies was appointed headteacher of Old Farm School, she inherited a group of assistants who were in the throes of industrial dispute. They argued about everything and anything, especially about starting and finishing times and who should do what when. Mrs Davies realised that drastic measures were called for if she was to get the best from this group. Eventually she renegotiated roles with each of them, defining them carefully and specifically increasing the amount of responsibility they had for helping the school to run smoothly. A year later, she had a fine workforce of assistants who contributed enormously to both the school and their class teams. She even had to chivvy home one assistant who was still at school at five o'clock sorting out IT equipment.

Although these assistants appeared to be complaining that they were being overworked, they were really anxious to have their roles made clear. They proved that they were more than willing to commit their time and energy to the needs of the school and pupils when expectations were clarified. In fact the headteacher had *increased* her expectations and this had acted as a challenge.

WORKING TOGETHER

Having defined roles and expectations of both teacher and assistant, the next preparatory task is to discuss working together. A central aspect of this is communication. How are you going to exchange information? When are you going to meet to plan? In a busy timetable, finding time for meetings can seem the biggest hurdle to working together. As with most new ventures, time must be invested at the beginning of a relationship. Specific meetings should be arranged with plenty of time for relaxed discussion. Ideally these should be timetabled as part of the working day and it is a measure of the commitment of a headteacher if s/he is prepared to facilitate such meetings.

If it is impossible to find time during the school day to discuss the way in which you are going to work together, then there are ways of finding time either first thing in the morning or after the children have gone home. If your assistant's hours do not allow for this, it will be possible to negotiate for him or her to exchange some hours within school time for some outside. Although, in the short term, this will take time from working with pupils, in the long run it will be time well spent which will save the need for redressing difficult situations if they arise.

There will be many other times when meetings will be necessary and time will need to be set aside regularly. Planning time is most important. Research by both Balshaw (1991a) and Thomas (1992) has indicated that one of the greatest frustrations for additional adults in the classroom is lack of planning. They arrive at the beginning of lessons not knowing what they are about, what their role is or even if there is a role for them. Consider this scenario:

> Mr Allen arrived five minutes before the science lesson was about to begin. His general brief in science was to support a small group of pupils with SEN with whom he usually sits. The science teacher, Mrs Rowan, was still gathering equipment and in passing just said that she was introducing a new topic that day. Mrs Rowan conducted a whole class lesson, skilfully involving all the pupils and preparing them for future lessons in which they would be testing things for themselves. There was no role for Mr Allen except as one of the class, listening to the lesson. Not surprisingly, he felt frustrated that time had been wasted.

This is not an unusual occurrence and it could have been avoided if planning time had been properly employed. The teacher could have ensured that the science content of the lesson was available on paper so the assistant had the information that the pupils had without having to attend the lesson. They could have planned together the adaptation of the material and activities which could have been the task for the assistant during this lead lesson.

CO-ORDINATING THE CLASSROOM TEAM

It is usually the job of the teacher to co-ordinate the work of the classroom team. This does not necessarily mean that this is a traditional leadership position with the teacher as leader and assistant as follower but is more of an equal partnership. Equal, in this context, does not mean the same but that each person has a voice within the team which is equally important. This kind of team is beginning to show great success in the business world. It is tempting to say that the human services are very different from business but there are many aspects which do have relevance. From manufacturing it can be seen that more and more teams are becoming flatter in hierarchy (as the nursery team in Chapter 1 was). No longer is it deemed appropriate for there to be an autocratic leader who rules the team with orders and judgements. The team that is most effective is one whose members take collective responsibility for decisions and problem solving. A leader is necessary but this is not a post with power over other members, it is much closer to the meaning of a co-ordinator: one who brings everything together and makes sure everyone has all the information they need.

It is not possible to provide a list of the responsibilities of a classroom team co-ordinator because that is something each of you will need to discuss and work out with your own team. This is not a stage that can be omitted from your growth together. I will, however list some areas to guide your discussion. Co-ordination is needed for:

- team meetings,
- records and reports,
- assessment of pupil needs,
- teaching and care programmes,
- planning pupil programmes, topics and schemes of work,
- passing on information of all kinds,
- working with parents,
- working with the SENCO, and
- working with other agencies and services.

Although co-ordination is needed in all these areas, it does not mean that the teacher will necessarily be solely responsible for them all. Teamwork is about sharing and there will be many opportunities for the assistant to take on the parts of the role in which s/he has the most interest. Consider this example:

Mrs Ball (assistant) has a particular interest in the physical needs of the pupils in the infant department. She has become the first point of reference for the physiotherapist who visits the school once a week for two hours. Mrs Ball has been trained to carry out simple daily stretching exercises with the pupils with cerebral palsy. These are checked regularly by the physiotherapist who teaches Mrs Ball new exercises when the need arises. There are four classes in the infant department and Mrs Ball works with a total of six children from all four classes and with their teachers. She also keeps the SENCO informed. She has accepted responsibility for co-ordinating the physiotherapy input and with the teachers has developed a record keeping system which is a very efficient way of communicating what has happened in exercise sessions.

Mrs Ball also works with the physiotherapist when she comes to school and conveys messages concerning positioning and equipment to teachers and to parents. At the beginning of each school year, the physiotherapist spends a whole day at the school, reassessing children's needs and discussing physical programmes with Mrs Ball. The final hour of the day (3-4 pm) is spent with the class teachers involved where these programmes are discussed jointly so that where possible they can be incorporated into academic work and everyone is aware of their purpose. At the end of the school year, reports are prepared and a final meeting takes place with everyone involved. Meeting times are a compromise with management providing cover for half the time and the staff giving the other half outside of the school day.

This is a good example of trust within a team. A few years ago the management term might be successful delegation, but within a collaborative team it can be seen as effective teamwork. An individual's strength and interest is being used for the benefit of the whole department. This may seem a subtle difference but it is an important shift which denotes the retaining of responsibility by the whole team whilst sharing out the work itself.

As this is an important point, I shall include a second example of how this might work:

Miss Lake is a full time assistant who mainly works alongside the two Year 6 teachers. For the last two years, she has been working with small groups of pupils with SEN. She works on basic reading and writing skills in an area set aside for this purpose. This is a well resourced area and Miss Lake has been trained by the SENCO to use these to encourage pupils with learning difficulties to overcome some of their problems. Planning is undertaken with class teachers and the SENCO on a half termly basis with *ad hoc* meetings at other times. Most of the sessions last for 20–30 minutes and are carefully timetabled so that the breadth and balance of the curriculum is not affected. Sometimes the groups are mixed ability so that the weaker members of the class have good models to copy in their more able peers.

Progress is carefully monitored and reported to the class teacher and the SENCO and although close checks are made, Miss Lake is trusted to use her own initiative in most circumstances. If she has particular problems, she talks them through with the team and together they find a way to move forward.

Sometimes in cases of withdrawing pupils for extra support, class teachers can absolve themselves of responsibility for these pupils. It is tempting to feel relief that someone else is solving the problem and get on with meeting the needs of the rest of the class. This is not the case in the above example. Responsibility remains firmly with the classroom team supported by the SENCO. A small part of the work is actually carried out by one member of the team but this has been worked out as the best use of time and resources in this particular school.

A final example on this theme demonstrates a slightly different way of using team members which worked for one class:

In an infant class, Mrs King (teacher) and Mrs Tough (assistant) agreed to support the pupils with SEN in this fashion. Mrs Tough was responsible for the majority of the class during daily quiet reading, one story time and one art lesson a week whilst Mrs King worked with small groups of pupils who had specific difficulties. The room was arranged so that small groups could work without disturbing the rest of the class if they were listening to a story.

This arrangement involved some training sessions for Mrs Tough but she soon became able to make well-informed suggestions during planning meetings for the lessons for which she was responsible. She was especially pleased to take on art as this was her area of expertise. It was not Mrs King's strength.

This is a good example of using individual expertise to the best advantage. Most people have areas with which they feel more comfortable than others and it not just sensible but essential that this is taken into account when planning the best way of meeting the varying needs of the pupils (Mortimore and Mortimore with Thomas, 1994).

TRAINING

As a group of personnel, assistants arrive in school largely un-trained. They are mostly women, many of whom have had their own children and feel they would enjoy working with other people's (Clayton, 1989). Many have much to offer in the caring field and know from experience how to encourage good be-haviour and responsibility in their charges. Training is a central issue. It is potentially very wasteful not to train such a valuable resource in our schools but who should carry out courses and what should they contain?

Fox (1993), OPTIS (1988) and Balshaw (1991a,b) have all been involved in local authority training for assistants working with pupils with SEN and have converted their experience into re-source packs or books for others who wish to run courses. It is very difficult to find money to pay for such courses but now that schools are responsible for their own budgets, they can decide that some should be put aside for basic training for assistants. This should be viewed as an investment which will be repaid many times.

Apart from general courses, there is training in schools to equip assistants with specific skills, for example behaviour manage-ment and early reading. There is usually sufficient expertise within the staff to make this viable, although there may be times when it is possible to send an assistant on a course or invite a con-sultant in to cover a particular aspect. Schools who value their assistants enough to train them well find that they become extremely effective members of the team (Mills, 1995).

However, it must be remembered that changing the role of as-sistants from the traditional dogsbodies who mix paint, wipe tears and make cups of coffee to full team members who share re-sponsibility for the care and education of pupils cannot be achieved overnight nor without opposition from some people. Generally those are the staff who feel that four years of training gives a teacher particular responsibilities and that giving a few days training to a 'mum' who is then deemed capable of teaching is denigrating this responsibility. People who believe this often have fears that arise from basic misunderstandings and they need time to see what collaborative teamwork really involves and its advantages over everyone working in their own small corner.

CONCLUSIONS

The Audit Commission and HMI (1992a) conducted a survey concerning provision for pupils with SEN. One of their criticisms concerned the use of extra adults in the classroom. They found that lessons consisted mainly of the teacher's talk with the class, use of video or demonstration of some process where there was little role for the extra adult. In a companion volume (Audit Commission and HMI, 1992b) they give advice which centres around planning how extra adults can be used most effectively. During this chapter, I have tried to explore what might be meant by this planning and have given examples from my own experience and that of others to make this accessible to students and beginning teachers hungry for practical advice.

Making a classroom team work effectively and enjoyably is a difficult task but it is well worth the effort. It takes time, often something which is in short supply in busy schools, but investing this time can create a new working relationship which proves that 'the whole is greater than the sum of the parts'. A good team is not just two or three people working together but an entity in itself which seems to motivate each person to give more than just his or her best.

REFERENCES

Audit Commission and HMI (1992a) *Getting in on the Act: Provision for Pupils with Special Educational Needs: The National Picture*, London: HMSO.

Audit Commission and HMI (1992b) *Getting the Act Together: Provision for Pupils with Special Educational Needs*, London: HMSO.

Babington-Smith, B. and Farrell, B. (1979) *Training in Small Groups*, Oxford: Pergamon Press.

Balshaw, M. (1991a) *Help in the Classroom*, London: David Fulton.

Balshaw, M. (1991b) 'Classroom assistants: staff development issues', in G. Upton, (Ed.) *Staff Training and Special Educational Needs*, London: David Fulton.

Clayton, T. (1989) 'The role of classroom assistants in supporting children with special educational needs in mainstream primary schools', in R. Evans, (Ed.) *Special Educational Needs: Policy and Practice*, Oxford: Blackwell.

Clough, P. and Lindsay, G. (1991) *Integration and the Support Service*, Slough: NFER-Nelson.

DES (Department of Education and Science) (1978) *Special Educational Needs: Report of the Committee of Enquiry into the Education of Handicapped Children and Young People (The Warnock Report)*, London: HMSO.

DFE (Department for Education) (1994) *Code of Practice on the Identification and Assessment of Special Educational Needs*, London: DFE.

Fox, G. (1993) *A Handbook for Special Needs Assistants: Working in Partnership with Teachers*, London: David Fulton.

Fullan, M. (1993) *Change Forces: Probing the Depths of Educational Reform*, London: Falmer Press.

Lacey, P. (1995) 'In the front line: Special educational needs co-ordinators and liaison', *Support for Learning* 10(2): 57–62.

Lacey, P. and Lomas, J. (1993) *Support Services and the Curriculum: A Practical Guide to Collaboration*, London: David Fulton.

MacConville, R. (1991) 'A support service's response to the 1988 Act' in T. Bowers, (Ed.) *Schools, Services and Special Educational Needs: Management Issues in the Wake of LMS*, Cambridge: Perspective Press.

Mills, J. (1995) 'A classroom assistant', in J. Mills, and R.W. Mills (eds). *Primary School People. Getting to Know Your Colleagues*, London: Routledge.

Mortimore, P. and Mortimore, J. with Thomas, H. (1994) *Managing Associate Staff: Innovation in Primary and Secondary Schools*, London: Paul Chapman Publishing.

OPTIS (1988) *Working Together; The OPTIS Guide for Non-teaching Staff Supporting Pupils with Special Educational Needs*, Oxford: OPTIS.

Payne, M. (1993) *Linkages: Effective Networking in Social Care*, London: Whiting and Birch.

RNIB (Royal National Institute for the Blind) (1992) *Curriculum Materials used with Multihandicapped Visually Impaired Children and Young People*, Report from the Working Party (MHVI), London: RNIB.

Thomas, G. (1992) *Effective Classroom Teamwork: Support or Intrusion?* London: Routledge.

Part II

PARTNERSHIP AND THE CURRICULUM

THE SCHOOL AND BEYOND

4

PARTNERSHIPS IN READING AND LITERACY

Maggie Moore

When I first started teaching I had thirty-five children in the equivalent of a Year 3 class. I was told by the headteacher that I had to hear every child read every day. Even without the constraints of the National Curriculum I never quite managed it. The best that children received was a quick check of their reading skills with more time allocated to the poorer readers. This, however, did not get them through their reading scheme very quickly, which was something else that had to be accomplished.

As I settled in with my class, the timetable and the headteacher's dictate, I effected a compromise. The system I incorporated involved an informal assessment of children's reading (transfer from infants had not included any standardised test results or reports of reading competence), using books available in the classroom. Children were then grouped into twos, threes or fours according to the books they were able to read independently, and thirty minutes per day was devoted to reading. Children read to each other in their allotted groups while, during the course of a week, I heard every child read by joining their group, sharing their reading and talking about the stories they were reading. Each child read every day and they all progressed at a steady rate through their books. Children enjoyed their reading, they made progress, parents were pleased and the headteacher kept out of my way.

This was the beginning of an informal, collaborative reading partnership where children had opportunities for periods of sustained reading in a relatively stress-free situation. I was at the beginning of my teaching career and soon learned that there was much more to enhancing reading progress and different ways of doing so (including the recognition of the reciprocal relationship between reading and writing), but all involving partnerships of one kind or another.

Most learning is a social process where individuals learn with and from others (Vygotsky, 1962). Wells (1987), for example, shows how language learning involves collaboration in the negotiation of meaning where talk in a social situation leads directly to learning. It is often, although not always, discussion with an adult that facilitates the learning process and develops the child's potential. New learning can be achieved through independent problem solving under the guidance and instruction of an adult or, as this chapter also demonstrates, in collaboration with more capable peers. Bruner (1977) refers to this social interactional framework, where children can learn in contexts and routines that are familiar, as scaffolding and describes the process thus:

> In general what the tutor did was what the child could not do. For the rest she made things such that the child could do with her what he plainly could not do without her. And as the tutoring proceeded, the child took over from her parts of the task that he was not able to do at first, but, with mastery, became unconsciously able to do under his own control.
>
> (Bruner, 1986: 76)

This is particularly so when developing literacy. An adult, for example, can provide guidance by encouraging the child to reflect on what is being read, encouraging re-reading when a miscue has occurred to enable the child to solve the problem and use the clues that are available to decode and extract meaning from a text. Such a partnership underlines the social processes of reading; a shared communication between reader and text and reader and other readers.

Discussion is often necessary when reading a book to determine an understanding of a text. It is important, however, that the relationship between adult and child is accepting and positive if a discussion which engenders a 'genuine shared activity' (Campbell, 1986: 166) is to take place.

This chapter will describe a range of literary collaborations which enables genuine shared activity to take place. The chapter focuses in turn on group reading, peer tutoring, paired reading and, finally, Reading Recovery, a New Zealand based initiative which has been successfully adopted by other countries, including the UK.

GROUP READING

The first point to be emphasised is that group reading is not about taking turns to read a book, following the text while other people read. The National Curriculum emphasises comprehension, response and interpretation of texts, all of which are accomplished more easily in social contexts. Teachers, therefore, need to make opportunities for children to read collaboratively, to discuss what they have read and reach a shared understanding of the text. Small-group reading offers opportunities for investigating a text and exploring the author's meaning in a social and supportive context. This enables children to interact with text in a purposeful and meaningful way at the same time as receiving guidance from an adult that facilitates understanding of text and develops their literacy skills. As well as dialogue with the teacher, activities that integrate speaking and listening, reading and writing, encourage dialogue and understanding between peers.

Classroom organisation

There are many different ways of organising groups for reading; these will depend on the purpose of the reading task. The groups may be selected on compatible reading ability, as I did in my first year of teaching. Able readers can be provided with a suitably demanding text, while less experienced readers would have an easier but challenging text which would need more support from the teacher. Groups may include a mix of reading abilities where less experienced readers can be supported and extended by their peers by seeing and hearing unfamiliar vocabulary read aloud or by listening and following a complete section of text. Group size is an important consideration: too large and not all children have an opportunity to read (some children may be too shy to read in front of a large number of their peers); too small and opportunities for discussion are minimised. An ideal number is four, with six as the maximum.

The text to be shared by the group is chosen by the teacher and will depend upon the needs and interests of the group. It is important that it is a text rich in vocabulary and story content; one that offers opportunities for discussion and one that can promote children's reading development. Younger children can have a single text that is shared between the group (many publishers now offer their Big Books which are larger versions of popular texts). Alternatively, groups of children may have individual copies of the same text and the teacher can direct the children's attention to text.

Group reading sessions do not have a specific format as they are geared to the needs of the group. Children used to group reading can organise themselves and make their own decisions as to who will read what or the teacher can appoint a group leader for specific sessions who will make decisions. Those children who are unused to group reading, or who are less experienced readers, may need more teacher direction. While other groups are working, the teacher can focus on specific activities which encourage dialogue between teacher and pupils and between peers.

Clay (1991) maintains that teachers can create a 'scaffold' (p. 265) when introducing new books to children. For example, attention can be drawn to the author, particularly if the group has read other books by the same author. This gives opportunities for children to reflect on other books and encourages expectations about the new book. The teacher can lead a discussion, encouraging the group to talk about the title and the cover illustration and predict what the story might be about. Inevitably, answers will differ, but the interaction between child, text and other children's ideas is an initial encouragement into the realisation that a book may elicit different meanings and responses. Children can share these insights and add them to their own book repertoire. The teacher may model the reading of the first page or two so that children can understand the context and hear an appropriate reading intonation. If the book is not new, but the group is experiencing difficulty, the teacher can talk about the plot so far to check that previous reading has been both accurate and understood or, if the book has been read by another group, invite that group to talk about the book and what they found interesting. Alternatively the teacher may read part of the text with or for the group to give momentum to the reading. In any group reading situation teachers can direct children's attention to specific vocabulary or punctuation. They can show how punctuation works in the text (for example, the question mark, 'why are we using this here?' or inverted commas for speech) to communicate meaning.

The teacher may encourage the group to read a page together which will give mutual support, particularly for the less confident reader. One 7 year old I worked with did not have the confidence to join in with reading *The Jolly Postman* (Ahlberg and Ahlberg, 1986) with his group, but read the 'pat-a-cake' verse when supported by his peers. Conversely, teachers can direct occasions for silent reading of a page and subsequently ask children to talk about the content of the page to their neighbour by asking specific questions.

Older readers who are experiencing difficulties may need their attention drawn to the range of strategies that is available to fluent readers. Many readers struggle because they have only one strategy to help them to unlock the meaning of the print. This is usually the strategy that has been given prominence in their early reading (Barr, 1972) and children have learned the strategy too well – to the detriment of their reading development.

Group reading offers opportunities for children to share strategies and learn from each other using prompts, such as:

- How do you know that?
- It can't be – because it begins with . . .
- It can't be Baby Bear Wolf – it doesn't make sense.

This group of readers in Year 3, described as 'struggling' by their teachers (Moore and Wade, 1995) were reading *The Jolly Postman* (Ahlberg and Ahlberg, 1986). Although the reading was begun by the teacher, children took over in a situation that was non-threatening and supportive. They corrected each other if a mistake was made and often gave an explanation as to why it could not be the word originally offered.

Children in the groups gained confidence to self-correct when reading independently, having had opportunities to read ahead and work out from the context what the word should be when listening to others and following the text. Further peer group interaction was facilitated through activities linked to the text which enhanced children's reading comprehension and increased their awareness about reading. *The Jolly Postman* reading was followed by a writing task where children wrote formal letters to children's television. This encouraged further reading and discussion by the groups. They read each other's letters and made comments: 'you can't say that, it's rude', 'I should put that in, it's good'.

The same groups read *The Trouble with Mum* (Cole, 1985) and wrote books in pairs that followed the same format 'The Trouble With . . .'. In order to do this they had to talk about the book, its characters and its format. They discussed the events they liked best, what had made them laugh and why and, in so doing, clarified their understanding of the story and evaluated its effectiveness. After reading the recipe chapter of *George's Marvellous Medicine* (Dahl, 1981) the groups read a recipe for peppermint creams and made them. In their determination to make sure the recipe worked the children re-read the text several times and frequently checked with each other to ensure understanding. Such purposeful strategies encourage children to collaborate, gain confidence and take responsibility for their own learning.

Advantages of group reading

The major advantages are that all children are engaged in a reading task to a degree that cannot possibly be given by a teacher to all individuals. Opportunities for integrated activities enable children to respond at deeper/higher levels to text, have better understanding of text when reading individually and aloud and make substantial progress in reading (Moore and Wade, 1995). Children have quality time for reading and for guidance from the teacher. They have opportunities for developing response to text by discussing plot and character with their peers and sharing their insights in a purposeful activity. In this way children come to a deeper and richer understanding of a text. They may become aware that in some books there is more than one layer of meaning (even very young children can do this, for example, in *Rosie's Walk* by Pat Hutchins where the illustrations add more complexity to the story line). Discussion with peers also encourages the use of book vocabulary ('I thought the second chapter . . .'). They also have support, co-operation and collaboration from their peers and from their teacher in a situation that gives a proper purpose for reading aloud; a situation that is very different from traditional reading to the teacher. The motivation that comes from collaborative ventures is increased (Lunzer and Gardner, 1979), as are confidence and self-esteem.

PEER TUTORING

Peer teaching is inspired by Vygotsky's work (1962) which states that instruction by more knowledgeable peers plays a central role in transmitting knowledge. Children may succeed in a task that alone, they would be unable to do. Whereas group reading encourages liaison between a number of pupils, peer tutoring is specifically a partnership between two pupils where one, a more able reader, listens to and gives specific help to another in 'co-operative working pairs organised by the teacher' (Topping, 1992). Their roles are not interchangeable. Unlike group reading, peer tutoring is not a partnership that continues throughout the school year. Many schools that adopt the approach do so for a fixed time which is determined by the teacher or project leader. Most interventions last for six weeks, with reading sessions taking place three times a week during which time records are kept of tutors' and tutees' progress. The fact that tutors also make progress is well documented (Topping, 1988) and negates to some extent the argument that pupils are being 'used' to help less able pupils and to save teacher time. Peer tutors enhance their own knowledge through revision and reinforcement when they teach; it makes their own knowledge more meaningful (Goodlad, 1979). Tutees benefit from one-to-one teaching, stay on task longer and receive immediate and positive feedback.

Organisation

Some peer tutoring projects use same age tutors; others use tutors from other classes. There appears to be no consensus of opinion as to which produces better results (Topping, 1992), although where the age and ability of the tutor is substantially greater than the tutee the benefits are greater for the tutee, but often at the cost of the tutor benefiting somewhat less (Topping, 1992). Conversely, an older pupil who is still struggling with reading may have reading skills enhanced and motivation greatly increased as responsibility and self-esteem blossom during a period of tutoring.

The primary school in which I worked found that, organisationally, it is easier for peer tutoring to happen in the same classroom with same age tutors. Even here, however, reading ability had to be taken into account. A two year difference in ability between tutor and tutee is generally accepted as suitable if purposeful and definite gains are to be made by the tutee. The school also had to take relationships into consideration; sensitive pairing by the class teacher or project leader is essential if the partnership is to be successful. Over-dominant tutors and recalcitrant tutees are not very successful.

Once the pairs had been chosen, the tutors needed training. It is essential that tutors are positive and responsive to their partners. They need to be encouraged, for example, to give verbal praise when appropriate. This can be difficult for inexperienced and younger pupils. Carl, for example, was so anxious to encourage John that he constantly interrupted John's reading, whereas Jane had to be constantly encouraged to give more than a monosyllabic grunt of affirmation. Both tutors meant well!

The most effective training method for tutors was role modelling of tutoring strategies, including praise, by the teacher for tutors and tutees. The role-modelling incorporated the strategies formulated by Topping and Wolfendale (1985). When the tutee made an error, the tutor was encouraged to signal that an error had been made (usually non-verbally, by placing a hand on the tutee's arm or shoulder), read the correct word and encourage the tutee to say the correct word before reading it in context. In addition, the tutor made a note of the word for the tutee to read later.

Advantages of peer tutoring

The advantages of peer tutoring mirror some of those of group reading. All the pupils involved, including the tutors, have sustained quality time for reading in a positive and stress-free context. In addition, motivation and self-esteem are enhanced for all participants, which in turn lead to purposeful reading where definite gains are recorded. Peer tutoring does not, however, offer opportunities for dialogue. There is no discussion, for example, about the book so that readers can share understandings and responses. The focus is on reading aloud to someone else for the purposes of progression rather than enjoyment and fulfilment. Progression is important, but it is important that enjoyment and fulfilment are experienced at other times in other partnerships. There can be opportunities for peer tutoring to follow the specific format of paired reading which focuses on progression, but does include discussion and sharing of text.

PAIRED READING

Paired reading is usually a one-to-one partnership with adult and child, but can be used with peer tutors (Merrett, 1994). It is widely used with parents and children, although it was not initially designed as a parental activity. The efficacy of parental involvement has a strong research basis (Hewison and Tizard, 1980) and is one way in which a partnership can be encouraged between home and school. This is explored further in Chapter 5.

Paired reading offers parents a more active role in their children's reading development than hearing reading, but does not give the responsibility of teaching reading. It engenders supportive and encouraging reading situations which are stress free, enjoyable and which provide the child with a model of fluent, accurate reading. Parents and adult helpers are given confidence by having a structure and format to follow.

First, the child chooses the book, irrespective of its difficulty level, from a range of texts. The reading takes place in a quiet environment. At home the choice can be easier; the bedroom is often the favourite place for children to read. At school it may be more difficult to find a room where interruptions do not take place. Classrooms can be noisy when everyone is reading aloud. After some initial discussion about the text, adult and child read the text simultaneously, similar to the apprenticeship approach advocated by Waterland (1988). The adult role-models by reading in a fluent manner with appropriate intonation, making no allowances for complex or unfamiliar vocabulary, except, perhaps, by pointing to the word to draw attention to it. If the child does not read the word the adult then points to the beginning of the word and reads it again. In this way the child learns more complex words in context by having the adult's example to follow.

When the child feels confident to read alone during the session, he or she gives a pre-negotiated signal, perhaps by tapping on the desk or the adult's arm. This signals the adult when to stop and when to start simultaneous reading again. During the child's independent reading the adult's role is to give essential feedback and the maximum amount of positive re-enforcement. When mistakes are made the adult points to the word and asks the child to try again. If the child has not self-corrected the correct word after four seconds the word is given. Similarly, if a child does not attempt a word, it is supplied after four seconds. The adult capitalises on any decoding skills that children have learned, but never encourages the child to 'sound out'. The adult's role, therefore, is not to teach, but to give a model, support and encouragement.

Advantages of paired reading

The one advantage that paired reading offers that others do not is that children choose their own reading material. Some children I worked with chose material that was far too difficult (for example, David, an inexperienced reader, chose *The Lord of the Rings*), but that interested them and motivated them to read. The support that paired reading gave enabled David to progress through a challenging book with understanding, enjoyment and learning. It encouraged correct and fluent reading, uninterrupted by hesitation, enabling him to extract meaning from the text. The reading environment was meaningful and stress free with no fear of constant correction and enabled him to learn to read by reading. Thus, according to Smith (1982), reading is made easy and positive reading habits and attitudes should develop.

There are doubts, however, about paired reading's strong adherence to behaviourist principles. Role modelling is obviously advantageous, but the immediate feedback and presentation of the word does not allow children learning opportunities except those of memory. Reading is a complex, cognitive, problem-solving process where the reader needs to be engaged at many levels. It is not a receptive activity. Children, therefore, need to be encouraged to solve the problems of an unknown word by taking on the responsibility of learning. In order to do that they need to be taught a range of strategies to help them: context cues, re-reading, scanning ahead, using grapho-phonemic knowledge, picture cues; and processing all this information to enable them to make a reasonable deduction. This may take longer than four seconds! Teaching these strategies is obviously not the parent's nor the adult helper's role, but encouraging their use could be. Encouraging dependence on one cueing system or dependency on the adult for supplying a word is not helpful for developing children's skills as readers. Never having the opportunities for self-correction, that is, the realisation that what they have read is incorrect, does not encourage children to take responsibility for their own learning or to achieve independence. Pause, prompt and praise (McNaughton *et al.*, 1987), where the listener allows five seconds to elapse before any prompt is given, seems to be a preferable strategy within paired reading.

If paired reading occurs in tandem with systematic strategy teaching and reading sessions where opportunities are given for children to practise their skills, then paired reading is a useful addition to partnership. If, however, paired reading has a priority because of constraints of teaching time then disadvantages outweigh the positive benefits. It is of little use being excited about reading and having positive attitudes if progress is not made in order for children to become independent readers.

READING RECOVERY

The final partnership to be discussed in this chapter is another adult/child partnership. Reading Recovery, recently introduced to the UK from New Zealand, is an approach devised and described by Marie Clay (1987) for improving young children's reading. In schools where Reading Recovery takes place children are screened by a battery of tests after one year in school. The lowest attaining children are taken into Reading Recovery (with no exceptions for behaviour or ability), are withdrawn from their class and given additional one-to-one teaching for a 30 minute period every school day until they are performing in reading and writing skills at the average level for their class group. This usually takes between twelve and twenty weeks, with an average time of fourteen weeks. The Reading Recovery teachers receive specific training for one year; half a day per fortnight, which includes either watching and evaluating one of their colleagues teach behind a one-way mirror or having their own teaching evaluated. During the course of their training year they put their skills into practice by teaching four children who have been chosen for Reading Recovery. During a research trip to New Zealand and Australia (Wade and Moore, 1993) I was able to watch several teaching and training sessions as well as interviewing participants.

Organisation

Each Reading Recovery teaching session follows a highly systematised format, but one that is geared to the needs of the individual pupil. The aim of each lesson is to build confidence, give positive feedback, reinforce previous learning and, after the initial lessons, to teach new strategies and consolidate learning. The overall aims are to enhance reading skills, encourage independence and promote confidence. Every session I observed started by building the child's confidence and encouraging success. This was accomplished by re-reading two or three texts which were familiar to the child. The texts were short, but complete stories, so that a sense of success and achievement was generated at the beginning of the lesson. After the known books had been read and enjoyed, the child read the book introduced at the previous session. This was read without help from the Reading Recovery teacher as the aim here is to check developing skills which are recorded by using a running record. This enabled teachers to analyse the miscues that children made and acted as pointers for further teaching. The strategies children used and the number and type of miscue were monitored. At the end of the book the Reading Recovery teacher often went over the story, pointing out any errors the child had made. For example:

Teacher: 'You read Mum there.' (pointing)
Child: 'Mother.'
Teacher: 'That's right. Do you know why you read that? Because you weren't pointing to the word, you weren't concentrating. If you point to the word you will read it correctly.'

Going over the story gave opportunities for children to self-correct. This is an important aspect of Reading Recovery. It makes children aware of what they are doing when they are reading and enables them to repeat the strategy on another occasion. As well as having strategies highlighted, children were given copious amounts of praise, both verbally and in the form of stickers and stamps. The next stage of the lesson related to letter identification (using plastic letters on a magnetic board) which were taught within the context of the book being read. Letter learning was then consolidated within a writing context. Children dictated a 'story' (often a sentence) to the teacher who wrote a copy. Children wrote the words of the story independently, were encouraged to use words already known and to expand what could be done independently.

After the sentence had been completed satisfactorily, and with much praise, a common practice was to put all the components in an envelope with the story written on the outside for the child to take home and work with parents. Although Marie Clay envisaged that this was a programme that could be followed without parental support, in practice (in New Zealand and Australia) parents were glad to be able to help in this particular task. Finally, a new reading book was chosen by the teacher to help with specific teaching tasks (perhaps an unpredictable story line to extend the child's strategies or one with specific vocabulary or phonic patterns to be worked on during the next lesson). The aim of this part of the lesson is to assist the children to put together the complexities of the reading behaviour and move towards applying the new strategies for reading and co-ordinating them with previously learned strategies. This is initially done with support which is only gradually removed as the child's confidence, skills and understanding grow. The book is introduced to the child by the teacher who will 'scaffold' by, for example, referring to the title and encouraging the child to predict what might happen in the story. A reading of the book is then attempted where all the previously learned reading behaviours are put into practice. The reading of this book leads into the next day's activities.

Partnership with parents in Reading Recovery has gradually grown in New Zealand. Reading Recovery teachers were anxious that the positive and supportive approach that they gave the children should continue into the home. Consequently, in many schools parents were invited to some of their children's Reading Recovery sessions. Many parents visited three times, at the beginning, the middle and the end of the period of Reading Recovery so that they could observe not only the strategies being used, but the definite progress made by their child. The interviews which I helped to conduct with teachers in New Zealand and Australia (Wade and Moore, 1993) showed that partnerships between Reading Recovery and class teachers were much in evidence. Liaison was strong between the teachers of children in Reading Recovery, but in addition we found that Reading Recovery had affected school organisation and ways in which class teachers were developing literacy. Reading Recovery teachers offered in-service to the school staff on some of the principles of Reading Recovery which could be used with groups of children in class; for example, explicit strategy teaching, praise and reciprocal use of reading and writing.

Advantages of Reading Recovery

The Reading Recovery programme is suited to the needs of individual children who receive consistent and thorough teaching of strategies which enable them to take responsibility for their own learning in a situation which builds confidence and introduces children to a range and variety of texts. Children stay on the programme for a designated maximum time; they are not forever in the remedial readers' group. Finally, it works! Currently interim findings for the English pilot study suggest that Reading Recovery children made substantially greater progress on all reading and writing tests administered at the end of a school year compared with a control group of children with similar difficulties (Institute of Education, 1995).

There are, of course, criticisms. One criticism is that of the withdrawal of the child from the classroom. In an education system where integration has been at the forefront for many years this seems to be a retrograde step, but Reading Recovery is not a permanent feature: the maximum stay for any child is twenty weeks. Another criticism is the cost of training and one-to-one teaching. The principals, Reading Recovery teachers, class teachers and parents interviewed in New Zealand, where it was first implemented, and Australia (Wade and Moore, 1993) maintain that the long-term benefits to children in Reading Recovery and for the school as a whole, far outweigh the problems of cost. They all refer to the progress children have made and to their increased levels of confidence and self-esteem. Many schools in Australia, for example, opted for a Reading Recovery teacher rather than having smaller classes.

SUMMARY AND CONCLUSION

In describing the four major types of partnership in reading; group, peer tutoring paired reading and, finally, Reading Recovery, it has not been the intention to judge one kind of partnership against another. Indeed, the list of advantages at the end of each indicates strongly the positive nature of each kind of liaison.

All the partnership techniques offer liaison between the reader and at least one other person in a situation that is positive and where praise and encouragement are freely given. They all allow support and/or collaboration between reader and partner. Although not explicitly stated for all partnerships, each has the opportunity to provide a text that is purposeful, challenging and of interest to the individual reader. Paired reading alone legislates that the choice of book should be made by the child, a consideration which is crucial if children are to be motivated widely.

Role modelling of fluent reading, crucial for some children to achieve understanding of the context, is specifically addressed in paired reading and can be a possibility in group reading. Progress is monitored in all partnerships, through texts and levels in peer tutoring and paired reading, plus monitoring of learning in group reading and specific development in Reading Recovery.

The crucial aspect offered by all partnerships is that of time: quality time without interruptions, time that allows children to settle comfortably into their reading, time that enables children to gain sense and meaning from the text they are reading. Other advantages are offered by the two, almost contradictory, partnerships: group reading and Reading Recovery. One partnership offers collaboration and support in a peer group and one is highly systematised and withdraws children from the benefit of shared strategies with their peers. Both of these anomalous partnerships encourage children to talk about the texts they are reading; to make predictions about content and story line, to offer opinions and begin to respond to the text as an interested and purposeful reader. This interaction with the text (and with others) facilitates a more complete understanding of what is being read. Specific guidance given by the teacher in both partnerships to develop and use a range of reading strategies encourages responsibility and independence in reading, enabling children to have the means to unravel the complexities of reading, further their understanding and develop as responders to books.

The great majority of reading done by skilled readers and adult readers is silent; reading aloud for adults is mostly restricted to parents at bedtime, newscasters, actors and teachers. Only one of the partnerships, group reading, offers possibilities for this important type of reading, one which is held to be essential for rapid reading development (Southgate *et al.*, 1981). Opportunities for sustained, silent reading should also be included in addition to partnerships. Reading, however, is a social as well as a private activity and collaborative ventures provide a natural social context.

Partnerships in reading of all kinds offer positive encouragement for reading progression. They also offer opportunities for enhanced time-management for the classroom teacher who considers reading to be too important to be restricted to one or two pages a day and who realises the confidence-building strategies of praise, encouragement, support and a good book. This chapter offers only brief descriptions of four partnerships. Referenced texts will provide more detail for enabling teachers to facilitate productive partnerships in their classrooms.

REFERENCES AND FURTHER READING

Ahlberg, J. and Ahlberg, A. (1986) *The Jolly Postman or Other People's Letters*, London: Heinemann.
Barr, R.C. (1972) 'The influence of instructional conditions on word recognition errors', *Reading Research Quarterly* 7: 509–529.
Bruner, J.S. (1986) *Actual Minds. Possible Worlds*, London: Harvard University Press
Bruner, L.S. (1977) 'Early social interaction and language development', in H.R. Schaffer (ed.) *Studies in Mother Child Interaction*, London: Academic Press.
Campbell, R. (1986) 'Social relationships in hearing children read', *Reading* 20 (3): 157–167.
Clay, M.M. (1987) 'Implementing Reading Recovery: systemic adaptations to an educational innovation', *New Zealand Journal of Educational Studies* 25 (1): 61.
Clay, M.M. (1991) 'Introducing a new storybook to young readers', *The Reading Teacher* 45 (4): 264–273.
Cole, B. (1985) *The Trouble With Mum*, London: Picture Lions, Collins.
Dahl, R. (1981) *George's Marvellous Medicine*, Harmondsworth, Puffin.
Davis, C. and Stubbs, R. (1988) *Shared Reading in Practice*, Milton Keynes: Open University Press.
Goodlad, S. (1979) *Learning by Teaching: An Introduction to Tutoring*, London, Community Service Volunteers.
Hewison, J. and Tizard, J. (1980) 'Parental involvement and reading attainment', *British Journal of Educational Psychology* 50: 209–215.
Hutchins, P. (1973) *Rosie's Walk*, London: Picture Lions, Collins.
Institute of Education (1995) *Reading Recovery in England*, London: University of London.
Lunzer, E. and Gardner, K. (eds) (1979) *The Effective Use of Reading*, London: Heinemann.
McNaughton, S., Glynn, T. and Robinson, V. (1987) *Pause, Prompt and Praise: Effective Tutoring for Remedial Reading*, Birmingham: Positive Products.
Merrett, F. (1994) *Improving Reading: A Teacher's Guide to Peer Tutoring*, London: David Fulton.
Moore, M. and Wade, B. (1995) *Supporting Readers: School and Classroom Strategies*, London: David Fulton.
Smith, F. (1982) *Understanding Reading* (3rd edn), New York: CBS College Publishing, Holt, Rinehart and Winston.
Southgate, V., Arnold, H. and Johnson, S. (1981) *Extending Beginning: Reading*, London: Heinemann Educational Books Ltd.

Topping K.J. (1988) *The Peer Tutoring Handbook*, London: Croom Helm.

Topping, K.J. (1992) 'Co-operative learning and peer tutoring: an overview', *The Psychologist* 5 (4): 151–157.

Topping K.J. and Wolfendale, S.W. (eds) (1985) *Parental Involvement in Children's Reading*, London: Croom Helm.

Vygotsky, L. (1962) *Thought and Language*, Cambridge, Mass.: MIT Press.

Wade, B. and Moore, M. (1993) *The Promise of Reading Recovery*, Birmingham: Educational Review Publications, University of Birmingham.

Waterland, L. (1988) *Read With Me . . . An Apprenticeship Approach to Reading*, Stroud: The Thimble Press.

Wells, C.G. (1987) *The Meaning Makers: Children Learning Language and Using Language to Learn*, London: Hodder and Stoughton.

5

DEVELOPING HOME–SCHOOL LITERACY PARTNERSHIPS IN MINORITY LANGUAGE FAMILIES

Adrian Blackledge and Jamila Aljazir

As previous chapters have indicated, parents have a crucial role to play in the education of their children. In the United Kingdom schools have sought to develop close links with homes to enable teachers and parents to work together for the benefit of children's learning. A particular focus of many home–school partnerships has been the teaching of reading. However, the development of such partnerships has been less successful in minority language communities. Schools have found that cultural and linguistic differences have created barriers to collaboration. The effect has often been that schools are frustrated in their attempts to offer an equal education for all children, and many parents remain helpless in their attempts to support their children's literacy learning. This chapter provides the perspectives of Asian parents in Birmingham, as Pakistani, North Indian and Bangladeshi mothers describe the strategies they use to support their children's learning, and articulate their attitudes towards literacy education. The chapter describes recent initiatives of two Birmingham primary schools with large Asian populations which set out to develop home–school literacy links; parents were asked about their response to these projects. The chapter concludes with a number of recommendations for schools developing such initiatives in minority language communities.

PARENTAL SUPPORT AND CHILDREN'S LITERACY

Teachers are sometimes reluctant to involve parents in children's literacy learning because they fear that parents' efforts, however well-meaning, may do more harm than good. Some teachers fail to include parents because they worry that the parents' methods may counteract the good work going on in school. However, there is no research evidence to support this view (Hannon, 1995). A second fallacy sometimes expressed by educators is that many parents lack interest in their children's learning. In fact, it is rare to find such parents. Most parents are concerned that their children should learn to read and write, and do well in school, but some lack the confidence and skills to support them. Some parents may lack literacy in English, for example, and therefore find it difficult to teach their children to read and write the majority language. This is not evidence that such parents lack the motivation to support their children; rather, they lack the skills, knowledge and confidence to support their children's progress in majority culture academic work. If parents seem uninterested in their children's education, the case for the school to involve them is all the stronger. Many minority culture families in Britain are concerned with the difficulties of coping with unemployment, shrinking state benefits and poor housing. In the face of these concerns they may not present themselves as active partners in their children's education.

The responsibility for involving parents in their children's literacy learning lies with the school more than with the home. Many parents have had unhappy school experiences themselves, and, therefore, find teachers difficult to approach. This relationship can only be changed by teachers creating an open environment in which parents are positively welcomed by the school. When teachers blame parents for their apparent lack of interest they are admitting their own failure to create a partnership for the benefit of children's learning.

Parents are children's first and most important teachers. They provide rich environments in which they talk and respond to children in a variety of ways. Many parents support their children's literacy by reading books to them, listening to them read, providing writing opportunities, and generally encouraging their children to read and write. Parents may support their children's literacy by telling stories and developing language through conversation. Literacy practices may be different in different households, but this does not mean that families with few literacy materials are in any way 'deficient' (Auerbach, 1989). The one-to-one home literacy model is far more conducive to successful learning than is the school model of one teacher to thirty-plus children. The most important role of the teacher in children's literacy learning may be to enable parents to become skilled, confident educators of their own children.

There is a developing body of research evidence to show that the involvement of parents in children's home literacy learning is an effective strategy. The most clear-cut evidence of the benefits of parental involvement in children's reading comes from a two-year study conducted in Haringey (Tizard *et al.*,1982). The project consisted of parents listening to children read books sent home from school. It was found that children who read to their parents regularly made significantly greater progress than a comparison group who were given additional school-based reading instruction. The Haringey study has been influential in establishing the widespread practice of teachers sending home school reading books for children to read to parents. However, we must treat the Haringey evidence with some caution. Four other studies set out to replicate the Haringey findings, most notably the Belfield Project in Sheffield (Hannon, 1987). None of these further studies showed significant effects on children's reading test scores when books were sent home from school. One of the factors in the Haringey Project which differed from the Belfield Project was that in the earlier study the homes were regularly visited by well-qualified outsiders who gave specific advice to parents. The parents in the Belfield Project were visited less often, by one hard-pressed teacher. It may be, then, that simply sending school books home for children to read to their parents does little to help those most at risk of reading failure: children of parents who do not realise how beneficial their help can be, or who do not know how to help (Toomey, 1993). Further, it is a mistake to believe that 'hearing children read' is a single activity which is always the same. In fact it is a learning opportunity which may involve a range of types of talk between parent and child; at the opposite extreme, it may be an interaction in which a parent is hostile, over-critical and responsive only to the child's errors. Parents may sometimes need support and advice about effective models of hearing their children read. Schools can do much to provide this support and advice, even in circumstances where parents do not seem to be readily accessible.

PARENTAL SUPPORT IN MINORITY LANGUAGE FAMILIES

When parents do not share the language or culture of the school staff the obstacles in the way of home–school partnership are considerable. Teachers are often frustrated by the communication barrier which prevents involvement of minority language parents in their children's learning. Minority language parents are, on the whole, keen for their children to succeed in the British education system. Many Asian parents encourage their children to become literate not only in English but also in a community language such as Urdu, Bengali, Punjabi or Hindi. Although some teachers may fear that acquisition of literacy in a community language interferes with the acquisition of literacy in English, there is considerable evidence that literacy in a minority language supports the development of literacy in the majority language (Cummins, 1994). Similarly, spoken use of the minority language at home and school supports learning in (and of) the majority language. The better developed children's conceptual foundation in their first language, the more likely they are to develop high levels of conceptual abilities in the language of the school.

A school which positively promotes the use of home and community languages is likely to reinforce students' cultural identity as well as increasing the probability of parental involvement. In the continued absence of teachers who share Asian languages and cultures, the most valuable resource for teaching children through their home language is the parent. Yet many minority language parents do not see themselves as partners in the English literacy learning of their children. They feel that their lack of English literacy and often their lack of spoken English proficiency prevent them from successfully teaching their children to read and write. In the Haringey study, however, many of the parents spoke little or no English, and many were illiterate in both English and the community/first language. One of the factors in the success of the Haringey Project was a regular programme of home visits by advisers on reading support. The most important lesson of the Haringey Project may be that professionals should reach out to minority families' homes to offer support and advice on how parents can best teach their children. This is not to say that in doing so teachers should ignore the many positive learning activities going on in the home; but parents may welcome advice on how to teach reading. Minority language parents have the right to know what white, educated, middle-class parents know: that sharing books with children is a powerful and significant predictor of school achievement. Not only do they have the right to know, they have the right to receive help in how to participate in book reading interactions with their young children (Edwards, 1994). It is not sufficient to say that minority language homes are rich learning environments. This is the case, but still many minority language children fail. Minority language parents are entitled to receive support in acquiring the skills and confidence to enable them to share in the culture of the school, and to enable them to become teachers of their own children. Classroom teachers must go beyond telling minority parents to help their children with their reading. They must show them how to participate in parent–child book reading and support their efforts to do so.

A number of projects have successfully supported minority language parents who previously felt isolated and unable to contribute to their children's learning. Ada (1988) reports a family literacy project in the United States for Hispanic parents in the Pajaro Valley, most of them of Mexican peasant origin. Many of the parents did not speak English; many of the parents had received very little schooling, and were barely literate in English or Spanish. The project grew out of an awareness of the importance of parents' involvement with their children's education. An important aspect of the project was a recognition that the home language is the best medium in which parents can educate their children. Parents were invited to monthly meetings at which teachers modelled ways of reading story books to children, and led discussions of the books in small working groups. The parents were encouraged to take books home, and to use them in a variety of ways, including reading to their child, asking the child to read aloud, asking the child questions about the book, telling the child the story as they remembered it, and asking the child to write a story. Emphasis was put on talking about the books in the home language rather than simply reading them. Parents were encouraged to do at least one book-related activity each evening. Over a number of months the parents became confident teachers of their children, and developed greater assurance in asking questions of the school and the District School Board. Allexsaht-Snider (1994) reports a similar family literacy project for Hispanic parents which emphasised questioning as the basis of literacy support in the home. Talking about books enabled parents and their children to understand that literacy is about comprehension of meaning in text rather than simply decoding symbols. This understanding led parents to feel that they were successful teachers of their children, rather than failures. The incorporation of parents' home languages and cultural experiences was crucial to the success of these projects.

Minority language parents need not be excluded from their children's education. Much can be achieved when teachers reach out to minority families and offer their support. An important aspect of this process is to listen to parents' concerns, queries and successes as well as giving advice. The next section of this chapter reports some of the views of minority language parents as they talk about their attempts to support their children's literacy learning.

MINORITY LANGUAGE PARENTS
TALKING ABOUT LITERACY

Eighteen mothers of children in two inner-Birmingham schools were interviewed. Eight Pakistani mothers from the Mirpur and Attock regions, and two North Indian Sikh Punjabi parents were interviewed in their home languages by a British Pakistani teacher. Eight Bangladeshi mothers were interviewed in their home languages by a British monolingual researcher, with the help of a bilingual research assistant, as a follow-up to observations of their home reading activity. Half of the mothers had received no schooling in their home country. Of the remainder, three left school at age 12. Most of the mothers were unable to read, write or speak English with confidence. Both schools had a structured reading programme which encouraged children to take books home to share with parents and to practise their reading. Most of the mothers expressed little confidence in themselves as teachers of their children's literacy. They cited their lack of English literacy as the main reason for their inability to help their children. However, the mothers all expressed their concern that their children should learn to read and write English, and identified a number of ways in which they provided support for their children's learning. These strategies included:

- sibling support;
- book-related support;
- home-language storytelling;
- reading in community languages; and
- providing reading materials.

Sibling support

Most of the parents encouraged older siblings to read with younger children. However, the parents were unable to say very much more than this about how the older children helped, or how often. Sometimes older siblings were too busy with their homework, or had to work in the evenings. One of the schools ran a 'Reading Club' at which junior children were taught strategies for reading with younger learners. A study by Jungnitz (1985) of ten Asian families engaged in paired reading suggested that sibling support can be a successful strategy in teaching reading when parents are not literate in English, if the siblings are trained in specific techniques. In an ongoing study of the home literacy support strategies used in Bangladeshi families in Birmingham, older siblings were observed to be frequently employed in book-reading activities with 6-year-old children. In half of the recordings siblings tended to treat reading as simply a process of decoding symbols, with little attention to meaning. Sibling supporters rarely praised the reader, and frequently attended to mistakes by intervening immediately rather than allowing time for self-correction. In a small number of cases siblings did attempt to ask questions about the text, and were concerned that the reader 'put expression into it'. Siblings were generally interested in teaching reading to younger children, but were unskilled and would have benefited from advice and support.

Book-related support

A literacy support strategy used by some of the parents was telling stories from school books based on their illustrations. This enabled parents and children to have conversations about stories; parents would ask questions about the pictures, and either create a story in their home language to tell to the child, or ask the child to tell a story from the pictures. In some cases the mother would use the pictures to guess the story, then the child would read the text and tell the mother whether her 'reading' of the story had been accurate. In this instance the child was developing the ability to summarise a text, and was attending to its meaning. It may well be that this sort of activity is more valuable in literacy acquisition than simply decoding the print without discussion. In one of the audio-recordings of parents and children sharing books at home, Kabir, a 6-year-old, read aloud the traditional tale of Jack and the Beanstalk, which he had brought home from school. Kabir's mother, who is not literate in English, but has some knowledge of the traditional story, listened without interruption. At the end of Kabir's lengthy reading, she asked him questions in Sylheti, requiring him to retell the story. Kabir responded in Sylheti:

Kabir: 'First the boy had a beanstalk.'
Mother: 'No.'
Kabir: 'First he went outside with the cow.'
Mother: 'Who did he go with?'
Kabir: 'The cow; he went to market.'
Mother: 'What was he going to do with the cow?'
Kabir: 'He went to sell the cow.'
Mother: 'Yes. Then what happened? What did his mum do before that?'
Kabir: 'They had to sell . . . no, no.'
Mother: 'They had no food in the house, you understand, they had to get money.'
Kabir: 'They had to get money.'
Mother: 'They had to sell before they could get money.'

In this example Kabir's mother is extending her son's comprehension of the story by asking him to summarise the text in a brief retelling of the story. In order to do this she is asking open and closed questions, prompting his response, and modelling a telling of part of the story. As Maggie Moore has shown in the previous chapter, this kind of activity is likely to encourage Kabir to read for meaning, and to give value to his home reading. In addition, it will further develop his narrative skills in his first language, and therefore in English.

Home-language storytelling

Many of the parents we interviewed said that they told traditional stories to their children in the home language, usually at bedtime. It is now recognised that story can offer a vein of experience richer than that obtainable through any other medium (Wade, 1984; Wells, 1987). A previous study (Blackledge, 1994) found that British Asian children place considerable value on these traditional tales. In the present study parents said that some of their stories were handed down through generations, while others were made up spontaneously. In either case it is likely that the stories contributed greatly to the children's imaginative worlds and narrative abilities.

Reading in community languages

One of the mothers in the present study said she combined several strategies. She was literate in Urdu, and to help her daughter Samira to learn to read she told her stories in Punjabi and then read them in Urdu. Reading the community language is likely to support bilingual children's literacy acquisition. Cummins (1994) suggests that acquisition of literacy in the language of the home is crucial to acquisition of literacy in the majority language. Reading in Urdu will benefit Samira's reading in English. In addition, Samira's mother enlisted the assistance of siblings to help Samira read in English; unlike some other parents observed in the study, Samira's mother was always present and attentive on these occasions. In this instance the parent was able to share in the English literacy interaction by asking questions about the stories, making comments about illustrations, and ensuring that siblings took seriously their role as educators.

Providing reading materials

Most of the parents interviewed in this study said that they had no English reading materials in the home other than those brought from school by the children. Some had one or two books which they used for learning to read the community language, for example a Bengali alphabet book. Most of the children were not members of the local library. Two of the mothers, who both felt helpless in their ambition to help their children learn to read English, took the positive step of buying their children books and encouraging them to read. Both mothers recognised the importance of reading and felt that they conveyed this to their children. The two women welcomed any suggestions as to how they might support their children's reading.

These data suggest that minority language parents are concerned about their children's education and are willing to support their learning by whatever means possible. Minority parents are using a range of strategies to teach their children to read. However, this cannot hide the fact that most of the parents interviewed expressed their feelings of frustration about their inability to do much to support their children's academic learning. The following section describes and reviews initiatives in two Birmingham schools which were designed to develop parents' competence and confidence as educators of their own children. The first was a school-based initiative which relied on parents taking up the provision offered. The second was a home-based project which offered support to parents who otherwise had little contact with the school.

THE ROLE OF THE SCHOOL: TWO CASE STUDIES

School-based partnership

A primary school in inner-Birmingham was in the process of developing its work with parents and community. The school was almost entirely Asian, with about 70 per cent Pakistani and 25 per cent Bangladeshi children. As part of its initiative to involve parents in their children's learning the school began a 'Parents' Workshop' for parents of children in Years 1 and 2. Teachers invited parents to come into the classroom on a Thursday and Friday morning to work alongside their children and take part in curriculum activities. Bilingual classroom assistants were available to support the parents and the teachers. Two teachers ran the workshop, while a supply teacher was brought in to teach those children whose parents were unable to attend. The workshop began at the beginning of the school day so that parents bringing their children into school could be reminded that it was a workshop morning. The focus of the workshops was initially book-reading, as teachers modelled ways of sharing books with young children. At first parents would look on as teachers shared books with their children, but after a little prompting they joined in, discussing pictures in their home language, asking the children questions and listening to the children read. Some of the parents learned to read English during these sessions, reading along with their children from their storybooks. Some of the parents reported having altered the way they shared books with their children as a result of the workshop sessions. Typically, this Bangladeshi mother reported progress in reading with her 6-year-old son:

> Before I went to the workshop I used to ask him to spell out the words, but they said to me if you can't read the book then look at the pictures and ask him to explain afterwards what happened in the story. Now we read at home the same as he does at school.

Book-reading was not always the focus of the workshop. Parents were invited to take part in activities related to other areas of the curriculum. On one occasion, for example, the children were to observe minibeasts for a science lesson. The parents' first task was to collect a range of insects from the shrubbery on the border of the playground. This they did with great skill, placing an exotic range of creatures deftly into microscope viewers. There then followed considerable discussion between parents and children, as together they identified, classified and described the insects on the viewers. The effect of these sessions was not only to give parents a glimpse of the curriculum, at the same time it made genuine use of their home language, and probably even more importantly, boosted the parents' confidence that they were accepted and valued by the school. As parents developed confidence in supporting their children in the workshop situation, they were more likely to support their children's learning at home. As they felt valued by the school, they were able to ask the teachers questions about their children's progress, and to receive specific advice. In the workshops parents learned from each other as much as from the teachers. They were able to model good practice in sharing books and initiating meaningful discussion of curriculum subjects; they were able to develop self-confidence in the security of their peer group.

Home-based partnership

A drawback of the school-based workshop approach was that only parents who were able or willing to spend time in the school could be reached. Some parents did not attend because they were 'embarrassed that I can't speak English'. Others had attended at one time, but now young children prevented them from continuing. At another school in Birmingham, with a similar population, some of the mothers came from the Attock region of Pakistan, and were in full purdah. These parents were unlikely to come to the school, so a school-based initiative would fail to reach them. The school set out to reach the parents by offering support in the home.

The project aimed to empower parents to support their children's reading, even in cases where the parents had little contact with the school, spoke no English and were not literate in any language. Funding was received from the Basic Skills Agency to set up a Family Literacy Project. The school's strategy was to recruit volunteer tutors from the local community to visit families selected for the project. Volunteer tutors were all women, and were all able to speak the language of the homes they visited. Recruitment of volunteers was strictly based on the philosophy that the project volunteers should be from the community for the community, rather than imported 'experts'. Some of the volunteer tutors were attached to the school through work, including part-time special needs integration assistants, a playgroup worker, a part-time classroom assistant and a dinner supervisor. Two of the volunteers were parents of children at the school; another was the aunt of a child at the school. Others had volunteered after learning about the project by word of mouth. The fifteen volunteers were matched with fifteen families. Only one of the volunteer tutors was from Attock, and she chose to work as a tutor within her own family. Therefore, it was not possible to precisely match tutors to families in terms of their home language, but Mirpuri volunteers had little difficulty in communicating with families from Attock.

The volunteers visited the family home once a week to spend time with the mother. The volunteers' brief was not to teach reading to the parents, but rather to enable them to develop confidence as teachers of their own children. Parents who have infrequent contacts with schools tend to be less confident in dealing with schools and with helping their children's reading development, tend to have lower-achieving children, receive less help from schools and are perceived more negatively by teachers (Toomey, 1989). This may be particularly true of Asian parents in full purdah, who tend to be regarded by British society as either oppressed or eccentric. By failing to reach out to support these families, schools may give most of their help to the high-contact parents, who are usually less in need of it, and in so doing actually increase educational inequality. The volunteer tutors in the Birmingham project used a variety of resources to introduce parents to strategies for sharing reading with their children, including simple picture books, books from the school reading scheme and materials found in the home. The approach to reading was not prescriptive: parents were not taught a specific technique (e.g. paired reading), but were given advice about appropriate ways of sharing books with children. Strategies (along the lines of those described in the previous chapter) included talking about books, asking children questions about text, retelling stories from pictures, asking children to write stories, and reading print in the home and community. The project emphasised the value of home and community languages in children's education.

Home visiting may be the most significant predictor of success in home–school literacy projects. Hannon (1995) identifies home visits as one of the main differences between the successful Haringey Project and the less rewarding Belfield Project. A large paired reading project in Kirklees, involving 85 schools and 1,464 parents, found that supportive home visits increased children's reading competence to a significant degree (Topping and Lindsay, 1992). For parents who have little contact with schools due to cultural and religious reasons, the effect of home visits may be even more significant.

Some of the participating parents in the Birmingham home visiting project were interviewed to assess its effectiveness. The parents all welcomed the project, and were positive about the tutors' home visits. None of the parents said that the visits had been an intrusion. The most important reason for the parents' participation was to develop their own English skills so that they would be able to make a more effective and worthwhile contribution to their children's literacy development. Although researchers may approve of the rich home language environment of minority households, parents know that long-term support of their children's academic study will rely on access to English. All of the parents welcomed the fact that the volunteer tutors were women. They recognised that they would not have participated in the project otherwise. Initiatives such as this need to be handled with sensitivity when matching volunteer tutors to families. The parents also found that the bilingualism of the volunteer tutors was an essential part of the success of the project. There was no language barrier between the parents and the tutors, and parents felt that as a result of working with the tutor their confidence in their own abilities had increased. All of the parents felt that they learned a great deal about teaching their children to read; they were now adopting some of the strategies that had been demonstrated by the tutors, such as using food packaging to encourage reading. The parents said that as a result of this their children had benefited considerably, and their reading was improving steadily. The academic and linguistic growth of students is significantly increased when parents see themselves as co-educators of their children (Cummins, 1994). This home-based project successfully enabled a group of non-literate parents to become more confident that they were able to educate their own children.

CONCLUSION

Minority language parents need not be excluded from their children's education. Schools have a responsibility to recognise that minority language homes are rich learning environments and that minority parents are willing and able to contribute to their children's academic success. However, this does not imply a *laissez-faire* approach on the part of the school. Many minority language parents feel helpless when asked to support their children's academic learning, due to their own lack of English proficiency and their cultural distance from the school. Schools must create an environment in which parents feel confident that they can ask for and receive help, and in which school staff will enable them to fulfil their potential as co-educators of their children. In designing initiatives to foster minority parents' support of their children's literacy, schools should:

- demonstrate clear, unambiguous literacy teaching strategies through home visits or school-based tuition;
- provide bilingual/bicultural school staff to facilitate parental involvement;

- emphasise the value of the home language as children's primary learning medium;
- provide appropriate reading resources for parents and children;
- listen to parents' evaluations of school initiatives, and act on their views.

More than this, and less easily definable, such projects will only be successful when the school's ethos challenges the traditional exclusion of minority parents. The goal for educators should be a genuine two-way collaboration in which parents can confidently find expression in the school. If the school is committed to social justice, and values the languages and cultures of its community, parents will feel welcomed, and are more likely to participate in their children's education.

REFERENCES

Ada, A.F. (1988) 'The Pajaro Valley experience: Working with Spanish-speaking parents to develop children's reading and writing skills through the use of children's literature', in T. Skutnabb-Kangas and J. Cummins (eds) *Minority Education. From Shame to Struggle*, Avon: Multilingual Matters.

Allexsaht-Snider, M. (1994) 'The social process of a family literacy project with bilingual families', in A. Blackledge, (ed.) *Teaching Bilingual Children*, Stoke-on-Trent: Trentham.

Auerbach, E.R. (1989) 'Towards a social-contextual approach to family literacy', *Harvard Educational Review* 59 (2): 165–181.

Blackledge, A. (1994) 'We can't tell our stories in English: language, story and culture in the primary school', in A. Blackledge (ed.) *Teaching Bilingual Children*, Stoke-on-Trent: Trentham.

Cummins, J. (1994) 'Knowledge, power and identity in teaching English as a second language', in F. Genesee (ed.) *Educating Second Language Children*, New York: Cambridge University Press.

Edwards, P.A. (1994) 'Responses of teachers and African-American mothers to a book-reading intervention program', in D.K. Dickinson (ed.) *Bridges to Literacy*, Oxford: Blackwell.

Hannon, P. (1987) 'A study of the effects of parental involvement in the teaching of reading on children's reading test performance', *British Journal of Educational Psychology* 57: 56–72.

Hannon, P. (1995) *Literacy, Home and School*, Lewes: Falmer.

Jungnitz, G. (1985) 'A paired reading project with Asian children', in K. Topping and S. Wolfendale (eds) *Parental Involvement in Children's Reading*, London: Croom Helm.

Tizard, J., Schofield, W.N. and Hewison, J. (1982) 'Collaboration between teachers and parents in assisting children's reading', *British Journal of Educational Psychology* 52: 1–15.

Toomey, D. (1989) 'How home–school relations policies can increase educational inequality', *Australian Journal of Education* 33(3): 284–298.

Toomey, D. (1993) 'Parents hearing their children read : a review. Rethinking the lessons of the Haringey Project', *Educational Research* 35 (3): 223–236.

Topping, K. and Lindsay, G. (1992) 'Paired reading: a review of the literature', *Research Papers in Education* 7(3): 199–246.

Wade, B. (1984) *Story at Home and School*, Educational Review Publication no. 10, University of Birmingham.

Wells, G. (1987) *The Meaning Makers*, London: Hodder and Stoughton.

6

NETWORKING IN ENVIRONMENTAL EDUCATION

Mary Comber

Environmental education provides a crucial example of how individuals can work together and support each other in achieving sustainable development. In this complex and inter-disciplinary area, teamwork is essential within and beyond the school if children are to be helped not only to grasp difficult ecological concepts, but, more importantly, to become active citizens, able to promote responsible attitudes and challenge political systems.

While the teacher is a key person who can link the school with the wider community, the children themselves can also be catalysts in voicing concerns and being willing to change their lifestyles. After all, they are the citizens of tomorrow and their futures are at stake. The case for schools being instigators of change and the importance of environmental networking is emphasised by Parry (quoted in Randle, 1989).

> Schools are part of a social system and as such are influenced by societal trends. Many schools, however, seem to work in isolation from the wider context of environmental groups and those who have a role in developing good educational work. . . . Greater cooperation and understanding between all concerned with developing environmental education is part of the management process required in schools and local authorities.

This chapter will explore how working in partnership is at the heart of environmental education: in its philosophy; in school policies and practice; in community initiatives and international networks. Indeed, it could be argued that successful environmental education cannot be implemented without such partnerships.

THE AIMS OF ENVIRONMENTAL EDUCATION

The aims of environmental education have changed from a narrow biological/geographical study to the more holistic, bio-political approach advocated by the UN Intergovernmental Conference on Environmental Education in 1977. The Tbilisi Recommendations (1980) in particular, voiced the following aims:

• to foster clear awareness of, and concern about, economic, social, political and ecological interdependence in urban and rural areas;
• to provide every person with opportunities to acquire the knowledge, values, attitudes, commitment and skills needed to protect and improve the environment; and
• to create new patterns of behaviour of individuals, groups and society as a whole towards the environment.

The Brandt Report (1980), similarly, underlined the interdependence of all elements in the biosphere including human communities, thus linking the planet's life support systems directly to human behaviour and decision making about development; it is vital to live in harmony with the natural world. Reflecting this notion, the Earth Summit, held in Rio in 1992, put forward the urgent need for a new ethic and for sustainable development. This demands, according to the World Commission on Environment and Development, structural change at both national and international levels, particularly:

• a *political system* that secures effective citizen participation in decision making;
• an *economic system* that is able to generate surpluses and develop technical knowledge on a self-reliant and sustained basis; and
• a *social system* that provides solutions for the tensions arising from disharmonious development.

In line with this, educators generally agree that we need a new paradigm for environmental education, with increased emphasis on affective elements, actions and empowerment, as well as cognitive approaches. Thus, learning needs to be meaningful and to move from an ego- to homo- and then eco-centric view of the world, local to global. Students should, therefore, 'pick up the message' through experience and involvement, especially by practising decision making, by discussion and empowerment by participation in environmental politics. It is recognised that good education embraces 'head, heart and hands'. The emphasis needs to shift from mere head knowledge towards developing responsible attitudes and appropriate action. This 'thread' extends beyond the acquisition of skills and knowledge as it demands that the individual forms opinions and discovers a personal environmental ethic. Children realise that collective, positive actions can improve the environment (Schools Council, 1974; NCC, 1990).

It follows that it is important for children to be involved in real issues and identify for themselves practical ways that they can move towards a more sustainable relationship with the natural world, through changes in their own daily lifestyles, involvement in community projects and, possibly, political action such as lobbying or campaigning. At the same time environmental education can be an excellent means by which the whole curriculum can be drawn together while developing critical awareness and co-operative group work for a real purpose.

Huckle (1995), however, warns that environmental education in the National Curriculum is constructed in terms of personal attitudes, values and actions rather than informed citizenship, i.e. it is greening capitalism rather than being either socially critical or empowering. The teacher's role is vital here in raising issues and encouraging a questioning attitude.

ENVIRONMENTAL EDUCATION IN THE CURRICULUM

Environmental education was chosen as one of the five cross-curricular themes intended to broaden children's understanding of the real world and to contribute to their personal, social and moral education. Palmer and Neal (1994) recommend a co-ordinated approach with emphasis on the whole person in the context of whole school awareness and development plans.

This is a tall order for most schools grappling with the formidable task of planning from a subject base advocated by the National Curriculum Council and with the pressures of assessment. Even after the Dearing Review, with 20 per cent of the time at the teacher's disposal for more imaginative planning, it is unlikely that the cross-curricular themes will have very high status as non-assessed elements and without the leadership of a subject or theme co-ordinator. Incorporating environmental education demands careful planning across the whole school, which must involve the whole staff, not just teachers. Parents, governors, the caretaker, administrative and domestic staff must all be consulted and actively committed to joint action.

The curriculum itself should embrace ethical and moral issues as well as practical action and involve progression through a spiral development and integration of subjects across year group planning. It should not be directed by the subject matter, rather the subjects should be integrated into the theme. Environmental education cannot be 'bolted on' to the statutory curriculum but must be woven through the topics or subjects as a thread which holds the whole tapestry together.

WORKING TOGETHER IN SCHOOL

It is essential for schools to incorporate environmental education into their whole school planning and to take a long-term view. As in other curriculum developments it is the commitment, enthusiasm and strong leadership of the headteacher which determine policy and instigate good practice. This is particularly true if the style of leadership is democratic and all the staff, children and members of the community are fully involved in consultation and the decision-making process.

Targets should be set within the school development plan to achieve the aims in line with suggestions made for 'Greening the School' in Palmer and Neal (1994) and Poulton and Symons (1995a) and children's concerns and interests should be paramount. The following recommendations can be made:

- The foundation for the policy must build upon and meet the individual needs of the school, stressing that all children are entitled to an environmental curriculum.
- Environmental education should be *about* the environment, *for* the environment and whenever possible *in* the environment. (Wherever possible children should be given opportunity to experience contrasting environments, e.g. by visiting the local area, going on a field trip or through school links or TV/video to bring a local–global perspective.)
- The school should develop the educational and natural

resources in its immediate area in order to bring the environment within the classroom and take the children into the environment.

- The whole school ethos should strive to develop attitudes which foster respect for and appreciation of the environment, perhaps through a school charter, e.g. 'looking after the building and equipment'.
- The policy should enable the children to develop pride in their local area and responsibility for improving it. (Through understanding of a local issue it is hoped they may gain a deeper understanding of how world conservation objectives might be achieved.)
- The policy must involve the wider community – not only teachers and children, but their families, local businesses, the church, scouts/guides, etc.
- The environmental education programme should relate to real life and encourage children to participate actively in improving the quality of the environment, e.g. recycling, tree planting, playground design, writing to an MP.
- When appropriate, outside speakers/groups should be invited into the school to enhance the environmental curriculum or assist in school development plans.
- Staff should be given training, e.g. by curriculum support services, advisers and access to environmental study centres and other resources.

Thus, environmental education should involve everyone in the school and beyond, drawing on the expertise and interests of both the local community and organisations such as the World Wide Fund for Nature and Friends of the Earth. The school policy shown in Appendix 1 was drawn up with the help of parents and representatives of local firms and other members of the community.

Greig *et al.* (1987) identify some 'entry points for action' in a school in 'Earthrights'. These include:

- questioning candidates for local and national elections on their views on environmental issues;
- campaigning for play areas;
- assessing facilities/access for the disabled;
- letter-writing campaigns, e.g. local developments such as roads, housing;

- establishing an organic garden / growing food for school meals;
- producing a school newspaper reporting local issues; and
- inviting members of the community on to school governing bodies and other committees.

Some schools have developed their own 'entry points', as I will now show by using two local case studies.

Kings Norton Primary School, Birmingham

This school has been a model in environmental education, winning the award of Birmingham 'Environmental School of the Year' in 1994 and two civic awards. The development of a coppice and nature trail in the school grounds along with a school policy and the curriculum has taken four years of hard work by the headteacher (who acts as environment co-ordinator), staff, parents and children.

The head, Lorna Field, has a strong commitment to the environment and has been the driving force in developing the school grounds. She says, 'When I came there wasn't a blade of grass and the school is on a busy road. I thought "I must do something with this tarmac waste".' The school decided to take over an area of 3 acres of adjoining waste ground which belonged to the local council. 'The first thing was to get rid of all the rubbish. We filled skipfuls and skipfuls. I wrote to the parents and asked for their support.' Parents and volunteers in working parties provided the labour for clearing sixteen skipfuls of rubbish, tree-felling and digging out a pond. 'We needed experienced people in management. I knew trees had to come down as there was no growth on the ground but I didn't know which trees to take out and which to plant.' The local rangers provided this kind of advice and also two or three helpers. Grants were obtained from English Nature for tools such as scythes and slashers, some of which could be used by children, for cutting the meadow.

'We wanted to give the children a better environment to explore and for them to be involved in the planning.' Children have been involved in designing a woodland trail; the school garden with a pond; bulb garden; rockery and bird boxes (made by Lorna's husband); as well as orienteering work on the coppice. With expert help from the city's Botanical Gardens, using word-processing and databases on the computer, they were able to produce identification and activity booklets designed for different age groups as well as creative writing and drawing.

Lorna explains. 'They [the LEA] wanted to put up three Terrapins, but I didn't think these were suitable so I did a feasibility study with the architect.' The result is a gabled structure in keeping with the other Victorian buildings, with energy-saving built in. The new building has given opportunities for an artist in residence to promote artwork in the form of a wall hanging for the entrance designed on the coppice with Year 5 and Year 6 classes. A father, who is a professional sculptor, is helping Year 2 children, who are doing a topic on 'Structures and Materials', to make sculptures out of the waste building materials.

Each class made a time capsule to bury under the new building for future generations to discover. 'One article was a book made by a Year 2 class using CD Rom, talking about animals we need to look after now to stop them becoming extinct. . . . Whales, dolphins, the African and Indian Elephant and the tiger . . . buried in a Tupperware plastic airtight container. Two children put on workmen's hats for safety and went with the foreman to bury it while a hundred or so children watched the ceremony.'

The project has also extended beyond the school and the science, geography and arts curriculum to the development of a history trail around Kings Norton Green, the church, public house and old grammar school.

When I asked Lorna how the policy developed she said, 'We realised the need to formalise these developments with a School policy' (see Appendix 1). The school policy statement recognises that people are central and that the total enterprise has been shared by the whole school: 'We will work together for *people* and the *environment* to make a better place both for ourselves and for the future'. From the beginning it was recognised that 'our children's future is at stake' and it is, therefore, very important to inspire children to look after their environment and to be involved in the community. Lorna stated that 'a concern for the environment is life long' and that 'children are custodians'. Lorna distinguished between the 'musts' and 'rights'. 'We can't include everything, but priority must be given to some.'

When asked about problems of vandalism and educating the local community Lorna gave some very interesting examples. 'Before the Coppice was taken over people used the right of way as a quick route from the pub to the park or to walk their dogs.

Now they take most of their rubbish home. There are occasional crisp bags and we have a litter pick every so often. There was a tramp who used to sleep in the dell area and leave his rubbish but now he takes it away!' Surprisingly little damage has been done except the recent removal of a dead hedge and lighting fires occasionally. Perhaps the publicity given to the project in the local press and the award signs on the front of the school have helped. Lorna explains, 'the teachers have had some difficulties in getting over different messages, e.g. trees sometimes have to be felled (a good management practice) and how to cope with negative emotions caused by vandalism.'

The school is also an excellent example of how a local/global dimension can develop through an international school link. This came about because one of the teachers interested in development education had been involved with writing a book on Mali with the Birmingham Development Education Centre for the geography curriculum at Key Stage 2. The school decided to adopt a school in Ghana and to sponsor a new school building. Letters were exchanged between teachers, children and the headteacher who was also the pastor. 'The children were anxious to send their old school books although they took two years to get there!'

Boulton Primary School, Handsworth

This case study illustrates how another Birmingham primary school took advantage of plans to demolish old classrooms to rethink its whole school environment. The school has strong community links and a positive ethos. Visitors are greeted by a welcome sign in several languages and in the entrance hall to the Victorian buildings are an array of awards, including a civic award and one from the National Primary Centre. The school rules are presented as positive statements affirming respect, co-operation and trust. Other displays in the library reflect an emphasis on social education, celebrating cultural diversity, and include photographs of musical/drama activities involving parents for a Bangladesh week, and the history and development of the school and its grounds. The school slogan, 'Working together, building for a better future', sums up the aims of the school. Not only has the school involved the wider community in school plans and events but it offers activities such as a playgroup, an afterschool club and Punjabi classes.

A major refurbishment, including the demolition of some buildings, has provided the money and opportunity to develop the school grounds and play space. The Landscape Group drew up plans in consultation with teachers, parents and the children. The children suggested that the original rectangular playground walls should be modified to include curves to form an amphitheatre with tiered seating and grassed quiet play areas. They were also concerned that the disabled should have access, so a ramp was substituted for steps up to a fort-like construction with timber walls.

The headteacher, Chris Leach, says, 'We worked to green up the school environment so we took this opportunity to create flower beds, plant shrubs and retain a bit of field as a conservation area.' The skills-based technology curriculum has been the focus for planning. Different classes each took on an area to develop as part of their technology curriculum map for the year, as follows:

Years 1 and 2 – the design of a Victorian herb garden at the front of the school
Year 3 – the nursery area for 'sow and grow'
Year 4 – a fenced play area
Year 5 – the conservation meadow area
Year 6 – disabled access to 'the fort'.

There are plans for the tarmac area to be marked out as a giant world map with sundials. A signwriter worked with different groups of children designing wall plaques and signs and students from the School of Architecture at the University of Central England are working with children on the plans for the conservation area – planting a screen of trees and developing a mowing regime, with advice from the LEA Environmental Studies Centre. A local scrap merchant has been involved in the school's recycling project. English Nature and Birmingham Environmental Planning have provided funds. There are also plans for maths and nature trails related to an orienteering course.

There has been an environmental audit and it is clearly built into the school development plan by the senior management team. Together with other cross-curricular themes it is carefully planned around the subjects. The curriculum co-ordinator implements the masterplan once teachers with subject area responsibilities have chosen the topics for each year group. 'One year we all sat down as a whole staff to identify different curriculum areas and to plan together. The result was published in the teachers' handbook. People now have the skills to do it again.'

The school is also committed to development education and has strong local–global links; indeed the curriculum co-ordinator visited Ethiopia recently as part of a Development Education Centre project on water. It has links with other local schools; it is a member of BAEE (Birmingham Association for Environmental Education), Learning through Landscapes and the Centre of the Earth as well as the Architects Groups. It finds the Local Environment Forum set up by the Council with monthly meetings open to the general public, useful for debate, and NAEE (National Association for Environmental Education) publications useful for networking.

PARTNERSHIPS AND NETWORKING OUTSIDE SCHOOL

Environmental and development education support

Some very useful links have been forged between local teachers interested in environmental education who meet regularly, arrange programmes of speakers, visits and provide support material for the classroom. For example, in Birmingham this has been through BAEE. Local circumstances differ, but in this city the Botanical Gardens, the Environmental Studies Centre and Countryside Parks/Rangers also provide advice and are actively involved in providing curriculum enhancement.

The Development Education Centre (DEC) has its own network of TIDE (Teachers in Development Education) members who regularly receive a newsletter, in-service training, or resources through the Centre. The Centre itself provides a focal point for meetings and has provided a link between teachers in development and environmental education, especially through seminars, curriculum development workshops, geography and science projects, and writing to produce teachers' books and ideas for classroom activities. As well as providing an outlet for teachers' creative energies the Centre is important in disseminating new approaches to teaching and learning through a comprehensive range of materials through its resources shop and information service. Through the work of the DEC teachers can tap into a national and international network of other teachers, curriculum developers and research. Similarly the NAEE (National Association of Environmental Education) and the CEE (Council for Environmental Education) link teachers interested particularly in environmental education together, keeping them on the forefront of developments, especially through publication of articles and conferences. Interestingly, the World Wide Fund for Nature is offering a distance learning MSc/PG.Dip in environmental and development education which draws on the expertise of NGOs (non-governmental organisations) in both fields.

The International Centre for Conservation Education (ICCE) produces a wealth of information on resources for primary and secondary schools through its Green Letter Filter Service, while the Royal Society for the Protection of Birds (RSPB) and Tidy Britain Group actively promote children's involvement in environmental projects. CAFOD and Christian Aid are two Christian organisations which produce useful resources for schools on development/environment issues. CAFOD's 'Renewing the Earth' campaign provided an excellent video and study booklet bringing a Christian values perspective to environmental/justice issues as part of its adult education programme. Teachers would find many useful ideas here for action and promoting global citizenship in this material e.g. awareness raising, recycling, campaigning, changing lifestyles.

ESSO is a good example of industrial partnership with education, funding school projects such as Greenlink and School Watch; supporting research; training teachers through placements; working with environmental organisations, as well as producing resource materials. Exhibitions and competitions are another way industries and businesses help environmental education.

Networking in Europe

Environmental education is being established as a component of the school curriculum in many countries throughout the world. In Europe the Ministers of Education of EC countries have made a joint commitment to promote environmental education at all levels of education. Agenda 21, the strategy agreed at the Earth Summit in Rio, reaffirms the need for the establishment of environmental education programmes. If environmental education is to be effective teachers need both pre-service and in-service training. Currently a great deal of development work on environmental education is being undertaken in schools and research and development is also occurring in teacher education institutions. However, these initiatives tend to take place in isolation. There is a need to develop international networks and to develop a research base.

The Association for Teacher Education in Europe (ATEE) is the leading organisation promoting collaboration, research and development for teacher education in Europe. The aims of the ATEE Environment group are to:

- establish a regular forum for teacher education with an active interest in environmental education;
- promote research in the context of teacher education and publication in the field of environmental education;
- develop and strengthen links with existing networks, especially EC and UNEP projects; and
- relate European environmental education issues to a global context.

The EEC are funding a new project entitled 'Environmental Education into Initial Training in Europe' (EEITE) with the aim of developing teaching materials and publishing and disseminating information through country representatives and experts. The Council of Europe has issued a recommendation on environmental education of great importance to environmental planners, developers and decision makers as well as to educators. It recognises the planetary dimension of environmental problems and the need to create an infrastructure to help teachers through the provision of consultants, training and resources, using creative multi-disciplinary approaches and new technologies.

Networks with developing countries

Networks between the 'North' and developing countries range in scale from high profile exchanges at government level to personal contact. For example, links made at the Earth Summit in 1992 led to delegations visiting Birmingham which were hosted by the City Council. This formed the basis of the Birmingham Brazil Friendship Link, involving exchanges through colleges, environment and development organisations, churches and culture groups.

MARY COMBER

At school level, Beddis and Mares (1988) make the case for class-to-class interlinking:

- To encourage and help pupils develop a knowledge and understanding of themselves, their families and friends, their local neighbourhood and environment, and their country using a wide range of study methods.
- To encourage and help pupils communicate to others this understanding of themselves, their community environment and country, and their feelings and attitudes towards them. This may be done in a variety of ways – through writing, speech, images, sounds, models, music and artifacts. It may also involve the use of electronic mailing and new information technologies, and offer support for the learning of a foreign language.
- To enable pupils to learn something of people, neighbourhoods, environments and ways of life in other parts of the world through the receipt and active study of similar communications from pupils of their own age.
- Through this deeper understanding to counteract prejudice, develop sympathetic and caring attitudes to other peoples and ways of life, and a sense of responsibility for the environment, both locally and globally.

Through such links children gain an appreciation of similarities in the basic need for shelter, food and water, health, education and family life, while realising that there are differences in lifestyles, even within one country, related to local environment, access to services and economics. One of the striking contrasts may be between rural and urban communities. Children in an African or Indian village may find it hard to imagine that children in Britain are not involved in carrying water, planting and weeding as part of their daily routine; while some children in a British city school may never have seen crops growing or been to the sea. Some children in a Birmingham school were amazed to find a thumb print of a builder, who was illiterate and unable to sign his name, on a receipt for building materials supplied by a charitable organisation helped by their school.

The Avon Schools Link International, based in Bath, supports more than a hundred curriculum links in sixty different countries. Data have been exchanged with schools in Belize, Costa Rica, Nigeria, Zimbabwe, Italy, Spain and Germany. Recently primary schools have integrated fax with electronic mail to produce an international environmental magazine.

Norton School near Stockton, Cheshire has set up links with Lenane School near Nairobi in Kenya, in an attempt to understand more about life in the developing world. Teachers and pupils from both schools have been on exchange visits, to complement the computer links already established.

An interesting initiative in Kenya is *Pied Crow*, an environmental magazine for primary schools, distributing ideas for resource conservation and healthy lifestyles through simple messages and cartoon presentation. It recognises that children can be empowered to take action, and are often the most literate members of the community. This could provide a good model for other developing countries (Osler, 1994).

Research – using e-mail and more traditional methods

Advances in telecommunications have made it possible for schools to be linked by satellite and to exchange information almost instantaneously. Beddis and Mares (1988) discuss the potential for cross-cultural communication in *School Links International*. Keep (1991) explains that essentially 'electronic communication can be used in classrooms for three different purposes: communication, collecting and sharing information and providing a setting for collaboration'.

John Meadows of South Bank University is doing some innovative research on children's understanding of ecological concepts using Campus 2000 and compatible Dialcom systems. Student teachers are involved in designing questionnaires used to explore children's understanding of terms such as 'global warming', 'acid rain' and 'greenhouse effect'. Responses have been received from Europe, the USA, Australia, and New Zealand. Teaching programmes highlighted the need for developing activities for primary schools and engaging teachers in curriculum initiatives. Student teachers and children investigate model icebergs, the effects of acid on seed germination, detergent on oily water and monitor pollution levels.

Palmer (1992) has explored environmental understanding in primary age children through interviewing using photographs of habitats and concept mapping. She compares samples of children in the UK with those in the USA. As well as revealing tautologies and fantasies she has shown a remarkable 'emergent environmentalism' in young children. Californian 4 year olds have quite sophisticated ideas on recycling explained by their everyday sorting of garbage.

Both these pieces of research raise questions of how teachers, especially non-science specialists, can challenge misconceptions, such as the difference between melting and dissolving; the greenhouse effect, CFCs and the ozone layer.

Children's ideas and awareness of these issues come, as might be expected, from TV rather than the school curriculum. Teachers themselves may have difficulty in understanding these difficult concepts. This is where specialist expertise and curriculum support such as the CHATTS Project (Children and Teachers Talking Science, 1992) at the Institute of Education, London University is most helpful. Unfortunately, most primary teachers, unless they take a keen interest in a professional organisation, such as the Association for Science Education (ASE), would be unaware of such projects or appropriate resources.

CHILDREN AND THE ENVIRONMENT

The final aspect of partnership I wish to explore is that which can be developed with children. The United Nations Report (1990), *Children and the Environment*, puts children firmly at the centre of the debate about environment and development. It describes:

- how even before they are born, children are affected by industrial pollution and the poor health and nutrition of their mothers;
- how children are forced to move because of conflict and environmental degradation;
- how global warming may result in a future environment radically different from today's;
- how children are suffering because of our choices about public spending; and
- how the international debt crisis is affecting the basic needs of children.

Timberlake and Thomas (1990) emphasise children's vulnerability in terms of their health, dependency and lack of status. Since the 1980s, despite medical advances, children's prospects declined, not only in developing countries, due to economic policies and the debt crisis, but also in the 'North' owing to health cuts, the widening gap between rich and poor and the doubling of the homeless in Britain. Recent links between asthma and air pollution from traffic have emphasised that there is a need for legislation and for children's voices to be heard. This raises questions of children's rights. Although enshrined in United Nations charters these rarely apply in practice.

It is important that teachers listen to children's concerns and respect their ideas, not only about their learning environment and the curriculum, but for improving the local area. Some children have drawn up their own charters. For example, children from Year 6 at Moseley CE Junior School drew up the following charter for the environment in 1992:

1 A right for everyone to have enough food and drink to live.
2 A right for children to have comfortable homes and no slavery.
3 A right to have clean seas and their wildlife.
4 It should be illegal for everyone to chop down rainforests and green areas.
5 No animal testing, test on humans who use the products.
6 No war or conflict.
7 Stop killing animals. Do more to stop poachers.
8 A right to have clean and fresh air.
9 A right to have a clean area/world.
10 A right to have no ozone depletion.

Others have used time lines to project their hopes and fears for the future; or used 'talking heads' or speech bubbles to air their views (see DEC, 1992).

The Global Futures Project, funded by the World Wide Fund for Nature and directed by David Hicks at Bath University, aims to promote a futures dimension to the curriculum. It is intended to help teachers and pupils:

• to identify and imagine alternative futures which are just and sustainable;
• to develop a more future-based perspective, both on their own lives and events in the wider world; and
• engage in active and responsible citizenship, in the local, national and global community, and on behalf of present and future generations.

UNICEF's *Rescue Mission Planet Earth* (1994) gathers children's ideas from all round the world. Their imagination and initiative are a lesson to us all. Included in the text are some examples of children's actions. One was a competition in Sydney for young people to come up with innovative proposals for new laws. The best were declared on Voice of the Children Day. Top politicians, business leaders and the media were forced to listen, but did not always act! In Strasbourg a mayor wanted children's advice on a plan for the town so he got schools to elect a children's council and an action programme came into play. This idea spread and the movement had impact right up to national level and on Italy, Austria and Germany. Politicians see it as a way young people can gain experience in democracy.

In the UK, Save the Children Fund, WWF, and UNICEF have produced action packs to enable young people to organise hearings where they can question headteachers, local councillors, police officers, environmental health officers and others in authority. Some research commissioned by the ECO Environmental Education Trust in two London boroughs produced a report called *The Green Maze* which analysed the type of enquiries and which agencies the public consulted on environmental issues. One of the findings was that children are among the groups most concerned about the environment, but the least well provided for (United Nations Environmental Programme. UNEP/UK, *Good Earth Keeping*, 1992).

As the following case studies illustrate, children in school can be involved in grassroots democracy in different ways.

Children's voices: political literacy and citizenship

A Roman Catholic Primary School in Warwickshire made a link between environment and development though the World Development Movement's 'One World Week' in October 1990, when the theme was 'Speak up for Tomorrow's World'. As part of their work to develop the school grounds and to set up recycling systems the children were involved in making valuable cross-curricular links and developing new skills. They designed rubbish bins and made fashionable clothes and jewellery out of plastic bags and papier mache as a technology project. Later, with other schools, they mounted an exhibition at a local church and invited local politicians, the mayor, their MP and Euro-MP to a forum where they asked searching questions about local and global environmental and justice issues. The level of debate and confidence of the youngsters was amazing. A fashion display, drama, music and poetry made the occasion both lively and colourful as well as challenging. This is a further example of how local primary and secondary schools can work together for a common purpose and how churches and community groups can get together to voice their opinions.

Advocacy and empowerment:
culturally diverse inner city school, West Midlands

This school has a strong multi-cultural ethos. Most of the children are Asian, of Mirpuri-speaking Pakistan descent with a small number from Sylheti-speaking Bangladeshi families, plus a few Malaysian and Afro-Caribbean children.

The school favoured thematic, cross-curriculum approaches which were often issue-based. The children were also encouraged to ask critical questions. The topic for the Year 5 class was pollution and conservation, covering mainly science, geography and technology, but their teacher wanted the children to develop an understanding of the democratic processes affecting change in their local area and to take responsibility for their own actions. The children walked round the area making note of examples of pollution. At a local supermarket, recently closed down, they found asbestos dumped in split bags in the car park. They took photographs and sent the evidence, with carefully worded letters, to the Environmental Health Department. More letters were written to environmental organisations concerning examples of noise, air and water pollution. A detailed survey was made of a piece of wasteland near to the school. The children decided that it should be improved for the benefit of the local community. They debated ideas for an adventure playground, a swimming pool and a wildlife park. One imaginative suggestion was for a new mosque where Pakistanis, Bengalis and Malaysians could pray and learn together.

Small groups of children interviewed parents and local residents, mainly women, in their home languages, asking them what they thought of the current proposals for development. In consultation with the Residents' Association they found that the land was to be used by a professional football club as a coach park. This was followed up by questionnaires. A councillor studied the children's proposals, models and plans and tried to answer their concerns. A visit to the council chamber was arranged and children wrote to the chairman of the football club and they entered a competition for environmental projects. Although they did not win or immediately effect change they learned a great deal about power, social justice and local democracy, decision making and research skills. Their personal development and growth in confidence and maturity was remarkable (Blackledge, 1994).

CONCLUSION

Environmental education entails much more than just raising awareness of the issues and problems which face our planet. It requires a determination to effect change through personal commitment, community action and grassroots democracy. Much radical thinking and imaginative education programmes are required. Effective teamwork, networking, research and publication are crucial in this process of dissemination of good models of teaching, learning and action.

The challenge is: Can we influence the political, socio-economic systems and encourage others from small beginnings to present radical but also realistic alternatives to the status quo?

REFERENCES AND FURTHER READING

ASE (Association for Science Education.) (1990) *Opening Doors for Science. Some Aspects of Environmental Education and Science in the National Curriculum for 5–16*, Hatfield: ASE.

Beddis, R. and Mares, C. (1988) *School Links International*, London: WWF

Blackledge, A. (1994) 'Education for equality: countering racism in the primary curriculum', in Osler, A. (ed.) *Development Education*, London: Council for Europe/Cassell.

Brandt, W. (1980) *North–South – A Programme for Survival*, London: Pan.

Brundtland, G.M. (1987) *Our Common Future: World Commission on Environment and Development*, Oxford: Oxford University Press.

CHATTS Project (Children and Teachers Talking Science) (1992) Katherine Hann, Institute of Education, University of London, Working papers 1, 2, 3.

DEC (Development Education Centre) (1992) *It's Our World Too – a Local–Global Approach to Environmental Education at Key Stages 2 and 3*. Birmingham: DEC.

DES (Department of Education and Science) (1989) *Environmental Education: Curriculum Matters*, London: HMSO.

Dufour, B. (1990) *The New Social Curriculum: A Guide to Cross-Curricular Issues*, Cambridge: Cambridge University Press.

Garratt, D. and Robinson, J. (1994) 'Opportunities missed or deliberately avoided; The invisibility of the cross-curricular themes in Dearing', *British Journal of Curriculum and Assessment* 4 (3): 13–17.

Goodall, S. (ed.) (1994) *Developing Environmental Education in the Curriculum*, London: David Fulton.

Greig, S., Pike, G. and Selby, D. (1987) *Earthrights: Education as if the Planet Really Mattered*, London: Kogan Page WWF.

Greig, S., Pike, G. and Selby, D. (1989) *Greenprints for Changing Schools*, London: Kogan Page/WWF.

Huckle, J. (1990) 'Environmental education', in Dufour, B. (ed.) *The New Social Curriculum: A Guide to Cross-Curriculum Issues:* Cambridge: Cambridge University Press.

Huckle, J. (1995) 'Environmental education in the National Curriculum – is it socially critical or empowering', *International Research in Geographical and Environmental Education* 2 (2): 101–104.

Keep, R. (ed.) (1991) *On line: Electronic mail in School Curriculum*, Coventry: National Council for Educational Technology.

Meadows, J.J. (1992) 'International collaborations in teacher education a constructivist approach to using electronic mail for communication in partnership with schools', *Journal of Information Technology for Teacher Education* 1 (1): 113–129.

National Curriculum Council (1990) *Environmental Education (Curriculum Guidance 7)*, York: NCC.

Osler, A. (1994) *Development Education*, London: Cassell.

Palmer, J. (1992) 'The development of concern for the environment', *Primary Life* 1 (3): 46–47.

Palmer, J. and Neal, P. (1994) *Handbook of Environmental Education*, London: Routledge.

Pike, G. and Selby, D. (1995) *Greening the Staffroom*, London: WWF/UK.

Poulton, P. and Symons, G. (1995a) *Ecoschool*, London: WWF/UK.

Poulton, P. and Symons, G. (1995b) *Let's Reach Out. Primary Handbook*, London: WWF/UK.

Randle, D. (1989) *Teaching Green: A Parents' Guide to Education for Life on Earth*, London: Greenprint.

Schools Council (1974) *Project: Environment*, Harlow: Longman.

Timberlake, L. and Thomas, L. (1990) *When the Bough Breaks: Our Children, Our Environment*, London: Earthscan.

UNEP/UK (1992) *Good Earth Keeping*, London: UNEP/UK.

UNICEF (1990) *Children and the Environment*, New York: UNICEF/UNEP/Kingfisher.

UNICEF (1994) *Rescue Mission Planet Earth*, New York: UNICEF/UNEP/Kingfisher.

APPENDIX 1: EDUCATION FOR ENVIRONMENT –
SCHOOL POLICY STATEMENT (extracts)

At Kings Norton we believe that Environmental Education is for 'people' as well as for the 'environment' and, as such, should have links with all other curriculum areas within the school.

Environmental Education should involve *everyone* within the school environment and beyond – it must enable everyone to understand that the FUTURE depends on how responsibly we act today.

Through Environmental Education skills, values, attitudes and commitments are developed within our children which can contribute to a growing understanding of the concepts of stewardship, resource management and sustainable development.

Our job is to encourage our young people to examine and interpret the environment from a variety of perspectives within the whole curriculum including geographical, technological, biological, economic, political, historical, aesthetic, cultural, and spiritual.

We must begin with the experiences that children bring with them when they come to school. We will help them to learn to study and to value what makes their own localities what they are (i.e. the wealth of history in the area, the conservation of buildings, local river and canal conservation, the Coppice, garden and playground environment, and the pressures of an urban society including pollution, overcrowding etc.); and the processes which bring about changes in them.

Our aim is always to improve the quality of the Environment. The development of an Environmental ethic should come to influence all practices and behaviour in our school for it is to do with REAL life; not only safeguarding but enriching the environment, the greening of our City, the conservation of our energy resources, waste disposal and recycling, reclamation, our use of resources and conservation of resources.

We aim to bring in as many Outside Agencies as possible concerned with the Environment.

We want to enable the children to develop a pride in their local area so that, understanding local issues, they will then have a deeper understanding of wider areas such as world population, world resources, global conservation issues and the benefits and consequences of science and technology.

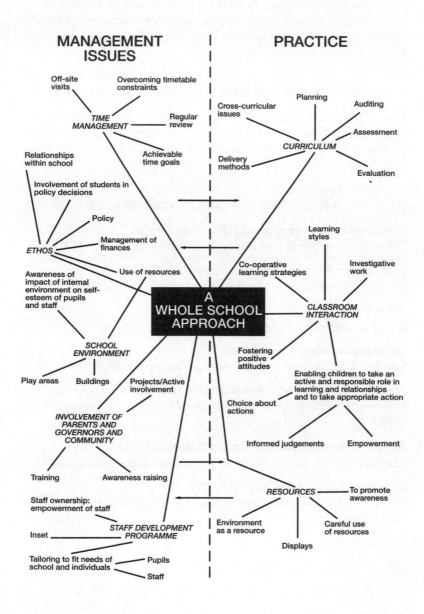

We will work together for *people* and for the *environment*. We shall make a better place both for ourselves and for the future.

At Kings Norton every opportunity for learning *within* the environment, *about* the environment and *for* the environment will be encouraged and expected.

APPENDIX 2: A WHOLE SCHOOL APPROACH

The diagram on page 121 is taken from *It's Our World Too – A Local–Global Approach to Environment Education at Key Stages 2 and 3*, produced by the Birmingham Development Education Centre (DEC, 1992).

APPENDIX 3: USEFUL ADDRESSES

Birmingham Development Education Centre
Gillett Centre, 996 Bristol, Selly Oak, Birmingham B29 6LE

Council for Environment Education (CEE)
University of Reading, London Road, Reading RG1 5AQ

Friends of the Earth
26–28 Underwood Street, London N1 7JQ

Learning through Landscapes
Southside Offices, The Law Courts, Winchester SO23 9DL

National Association for Environment Education (NAEE)
University of Wolverhampton, Walsall Campus, Gorway, Walsall WS1 3BD

Royal Society for Nature Conservation (RSNC)
The Green, Witham Park, Waterside, South Lincoln LN5 7JR

World Wide Fund for Nature (WWF)
Panda House, Weyside Park, Catteshall Lane, Godalming, Surrey GU7 1XR

Part III

THE SHOCK OF
THE NEW

PARTNERSHIPS FROM OUTSIDE

7

THE PARTNERS' TALE
Teachers, tutors, students
Jean Mills

No one who has had contact with teacher training recently can have failed to notice the preoccupation with 'partnership schemes'. Through these schemes teachers play an increasingly important role in initial teaching training, tutors talk possessively of 'our partnership schools', and students are 'mentored' on placements over sustained periods in the same school. As usual, change brings with it the feeling, as in *Juno and the Paycock*, that 'the world is in a state of chassis'. While much of the pressure for such developments is a result of government policy that there should be an 'increased contribution of partner schools to teacher training' (DFE, 1992: 4), participating schools and colleges have very often welcomed the chance to develop existing relationships. Accompanying these innovations has been a proliferation of mentoring and partnership courses, conferences, journals, training packs, videos, articles and books.

Naturally, increasing school-based training automatically brings with it alterations in responsibilities and re-negotiation of roles, whether there is formal mentor training or not. According to an HMI report: 'The idea of partnership is crucial to the concept of school-based training. The extent to which a course is school-based cannot be determined adequately just by counting the hours students spend in school; the more influential role for teachers implied by the criteria needs to be evident too' (HMI, 1991: 6). Such partnerships, however, are not like marriages, with two sides, a school and a college; they are triangular, with teachers, tutors and students having varying perceptions of the relationship. This chapter discusses the views of each side of the triangle involved in a training partnership for first-year students.

CONTEXT

The school experience partnership described here evolved from 1991 onwards between Westhill College and schools in the adjacent West Midlands conurbation. Intakes to the B.Ed. degree have fluctuated, according to government criteria, but one year some 200 students were involved in thirty-nine schools. As a developing initiative, the experience was monitored closely by me and the other tutors involved, and this chapter draws particularly on my evaluation of students' written and oral responses. For this part of the course half of the students' time was spent in college on education, and the curriculum areas of maths, English and science, and half on a one day a week placement in school over two terms. The experience culminated in a two week block placement in the summer term. During college sessions the students were guided in tasks which they completed in school (such as teaching three consecutive maths lessons to a small group; planning and teaching poetry writing; observing the school's policy on behaviour management). In school they assisted and were guided by their teacher. An education tutor taught a group of approximately thirty-six students in college, and visited them regularly in school, acting as liaison for around six schools.

Students were placed in class as a pair and expected to work together. In the early weeks of the course they chose their own partner. From the college's point of view this was done to support the less confident students and to ensure that from the beginning collaborative working was a formal requirement. Thus, during the placement one student could observe the other teaching, then provide feedback, and planning and preparing joint tasks could be shared.

TEACHERS' PERSPECTIVES

Teachers' perceptions of their developing role in the project were collected by face to face interviews and written questionnaire. Naturally, a notion of their professional role informs the way they approach supporting students, just as it informs their teaching in general. There are several aspects to this which I will outline below.

The 'good student'

First, it is clear that explicitly or implicitly teachers have a concept of what constitutes a 'good' student. This is related to those qualities that they value in themselves and colleagues – what Fish has called 'the moral dimension to professionalism' (1995: 34). More particularly, these are qualities that ensure the smooth running of the school without great disruption. The attributes of 'good students' cited by these partnership teachers were that they were:

- dependable (they were 'reliable', 'good time-keepers', 'well-prepared');
- co-operative (they 'fitted in with the school's ethos');
- flexible ('they were able to adapt their tasks to the school's requirements'); and
- supportive (they were 'helpful', 'I appreciated the extra help').

As students are temporary members of the school community, teachers look for and appreciate signals both that they will fit in and show commitment. They try to assess whether they have a 'good student'. June, talking of her two students, Simon and Kathy, said, 'they presented themselves at first as friendly, interested but above all confident. . . . After five day visits they were becoming sensitive to the demands that I and the children were making on them. They were also determined to give a good impression'. Another teacher, Paul, noted of his students, Audrey and Sonia, 'they ask for advice and take guidance'. Instances of helping with the Christmas fair, going on the Outward Bound weekend, staying after school to put up a display unprompted, chasing and, moreover, retrieving a runaway unbidden on a school trip, were all spoken of with approbation. Conversely, teachers' confidence in students was undermined by those who appeared 'laid back and lacking in initiative', fumbling in the dark', 'vague and unclear of what was required'. Teachers look for a 'good fit'.

Developing a role

Secondly, although the college has outlined the role it wishes them to take on, teachers develop and interpret that role in their own way and according to their own circumstances. They adapt themselves for the task. In turn they signal their commitment to this role by actually volunteering to have students and by talking of 'my students'. So, for some teachers and schools it is not a case of students simply conforming to practice in one class, the approach and ethos of the whole school is important, and it is a common procedure in many schools for a designated teacher to talk to students early on about expectations, and for there to be written guidance. That from Dodford School states:

> We feel strongly that all students who come to Dodford school are here to observe, to question, to learn, to contribute and to gain experience of working in a multi-cultural Primary School and that the staff as a whole will do their best to enable this to happen. While you are working in school you will be treated as a professional and as such we would expect the following. . . .

While these generally involve conventional but significant aspects, such as the school's dress code, phoning in absences, how to use the staffroom, access to resources, respecting confidentiality, they also vary according to the priorities of a school. Thus, at Fordingly J.I. students are asked to learn and apply the school's policy on assertive discipline; at Encarta the students are advised how to be positive and encouraging with all the children; at Maple lunchtime equal opportunities sessions are laid on to convey the children's languages and culture and how these affect the curriculum.

Again, although the college asks that students have certain basic experiences if this is possible for a school, such as visiting another class or age range, many teachers clearly go well beyond this in arranging a series of events. These might be observing particular lessons, such as percussion, or ensuring that all students in a school observe in each other's classes and then meet as a group for a feedback session. Such 'extras' and giving a lot of time during lunch hours and after school for discussion are aspects that make students feel welcomed and valued, with their training taken seriously by their teachers. Similarly, teachers become the students' advocates, judging when they may be too diffident or inexperienced to advertise their own work. 'Did they tell you that they took the whole class yesterday?' 'Have you seen their display, they spent all afternoon on it?' 'Oh, if only you'd come earlier, you'd have seen our teddy bears' picnic.'

These signals of commitment, then, seem to be an ingredient

for a successful partnership. A further one, suggested by the previous comments, is the ability to observe and reflect on the process. In the early stages of the project there was a contrast between teachers who took time to interpret the behaviour of their students and those who rushed to judgement. Thus, some teachers criticised students who, after a term in college, had, apparently, low expectations of children in an inner city school, did not realise what was evidence of emergent writing, or 'appeared laid back'. In Fish's words, 'a willingness to investigate, reflect upon and refine one's theories and practices provide a better base from which to work with student teachers than the unfounded and quickly punctured certainty that springs from ignorance of the complexities' (1995: ix).

Other teachers built up their observations, just as they would with children. 'At first they appeared lacking in initiative and kept in the background. Now (week 10) they get on with their tasks and look for situations where they can be helpful. Their confidence is clearly building up.' 'There has been a marked change over a term and a half. At first they held back, obsessed with their tasks and appeared overwhelmed. Now (week 12) they join in, supporting and interacting naturally with the children. They volunteer to do activities.'

Over one term June observed with interest and pleasure the development of Simon and Kathy.

They immediately began to learn the children's names, discover their interests and ask about their backgrounds. . . . They did not cower, when, after a week, I asked them to bring the group activities to a close while I took a phone call. Their delight in this delegated power was obvious and I was pleased that they appeared quick and eager to assume control. The children were all sitting quietly at their desks with their arms folded, waiting to be dismissed for lunch. Simon and Kathy bore the 'expression of authority' on their faces and the children were reacting suitably. By the third visit I asked them to prepare an activity in Science for a group of children. It quickly became obvious that they had little or no idea about the National Curriculum and to be fair to them I would have been surprised if they had.

Their final assignment before the Christmas break was a spontaneous spin off from a Religious Education lesson they

were observing in class. I asked the two students to collaborate on a role play drama depicting the story the children had just heard. Simon and Kathy were very involved
and found that an activity such as this did far more to bond
them to the class than anything they had done so far. The
idea of a teacher 'as a kind of lecturer who gives lessons'
was evaporating. As Simon said, 'I'm beginning to feel a bit
more like a teacher'. They were very concerned as to how I
saw their performance as teachers. They would look across
the room to establish eye-contact and ask the unspoken
question, 'Am I doing O.K.?' But more importantly, they
were beginning to evaluate themselves.

Allied with this ability to make sense of the students' behaviour
was the understanding that observation developed their own
teaching. As June remarked of her own first practice, 'Surely I
could do as well, if not better than she did? Twenty years later,
with the benefit of experience, hindsight and self-knowledge, the
overview is vastly different. I can now appreciate her skill as
a practitioner and wish that on the few occasions offered, I'd
observed her more closely.' As Kate Jacques (1993) notes: 'Transmitting practice and also principles to another adult is not a
simple business. Mentors recognise quickly that there is more to
successful training and education than simply dealing with
skills.'

Similarly, there was an appreciation that working with students caused them to evaluate their own practice. 'It sharpens
teachers' skills as they need to analyse task setting, pupil response, methodology accurately.' 'Staff have been evaluating our
practice in the light of student observations.' 'Descriptions of our
work and explanations of our thinking keep us on our toes.'
'It helped with my professional development and improved my
organisational skills.' Thus, in successful partnerships, teachers
appreciated what students brought with them as well as being
prepared to put in a lot themselves. 'We have benefited from
students' ideas, enthusiasms.' 'Students brought in fresh ideas
which were enjoyed by the class.' 'I have particularly enjoyed
working with the students, it has been a valuable opportunity
in my professional development and both students have given
me ideas which I will be continuing or following up in the
future.'

TUTORS' PERSPECTIVES

As with the teachers, tutors' roles also evolved during the project. This was partly as a result of their own perceptions of what that role should be, but also occurred because of the way they were 'positioned' by teacher and student expectations. Some of these roles were as follows:

College representative

As an outsider, entering some schools as a relative stranger and others as a familiar face, one encounters a range of reactions. One's role can often be that of a sounding board, as teachers unburden themselves over their reactions to the latest government policies, or their concerns over the number of special needs children in their class.

The other side of the coin in partnership schools is that as tutor one is the recipient of goodwill that has been built up over years. For example, when I phoned a school to check if a tutor could visit to take photographs, the secretary said, 'Oh there'll be no problem, he's almost part of the school'. Schools went to endless trouble to accommodate last minute changes and match students to teachers. For a successful experience for all parties one key is clearly the quality of the relationship. This relationship, in turn, is dependent on clear communication, both written and face-to-face. Messages do not get through if the channel is blocked by prejudice, misconceptions, or point scoring.

The most productive discussions I have had were those conducted in a spirit of professional tolerance, humour and mutual respect. In these forums major issues, such as accommodating the school's ethos of active learning to the students' perceptions of death by worksheet, were negotiated. Minor disgruntlements of school life, such as overuse of the photocopier and startled teachers discovering that their every word was being written down by assiduous students, were viewed, in these receptive schools, as human foibles to be resolved, not as personality defects that warranted disbarment from the profession. As Haggar *et al.* (1993: 22) point out, 'Not knowing the intricacies of the staff-room coffee arrangements does not make them thoroughly inadequate and ignorant'.

Go-between

Once in school, a tutor operates entirely on someone else's territory. This feeling can be reinforced by the fact that there may be
nowhere to leave your possessions. Thus, in one school, I was referred to by two boys as 'the woman with the handbag', and attempts to put my coat in unobtrusive places resulted in it ending
up in lost property or the dressing-up box. Similarly, schools are
often short of space and it can be difficult to find a quiet corner to
have sensitive discussions with students. One obviously cannot
tell members of staff not to enter their own staffroom when you
are half way through counselling an emotional student. Starting
college work straight from teaching in school, I was struck, also,
by the fact that, whereas before I had always known where to sit
in a classroom, now this was no longer clear, and some teachers
clearly felt that one's visit was an encroachment.

This is partly a result of crossing that invisible line between
being a teacher and becoming a tutor. However recent and however long one's teaching experience, you are no longer regarded
by some teachers as 'one of us' but as 'one of them', an evaluator
and assessor. Thus, while your view as tutor is that you have been
observing the students, the teacher's remarks can reveal that she
thinks you have been watching and judging her: 'I don't bother
with that positive reinforcement I was taught in college'. 'I'd like
to see someone else do any better!' One becomes cautious of well-
intentioned remarks being mis-interpreted and welcomes visits to
those schools where the relationship has built up over time and
the wariness has gone.

It is my experience also, that students and teachers in the partnership scheme wanted the tutor as mediator. For teachers this
may be that the tutor conveyed or reinforced unpalatable messages. 'Delivering criticism and assessing students can be more
difficult than anticipated' (Jacques, 1993). They may have become
weary of continually suggesting ideas to, apparently, unimagina-
tive students, telling them to tidy up or come out of the staffroom.
After several weeks of not so subtle hints the tutor may be
brought in to put the teacher's point of view, and to discover the
students'. This, of course, may be that they feel they are very helpful, but they are shy, lacking in confidence, and, straight from
school, in awe of these confident professionals.

At this point the tutor needs to be advocate for the students.

Like barristers, knowledge of case precedence helps. After a little experience one realises that similar problems occur across a range of schools. This is a further way in which the tutor's expertise complements that of the teacher, as it is 'necessarily generalised across contexts and aims to be as explicit and as objective as possible' (Haggar *et al.*, 1993: 9). The tutor may be able to clear up misunderstandings. For example, while her teacher thought that Asha had left early because she was not committed, Asha was frightened of waiting on her own on a dark, lonely station platform. Other students thought that they were being asked to take on too much, preparing work for the whole class in the first two weeks of their placement, yet felt unable to confront their teacher.

Support

Although it was clear that the partnership gave teachers insight into students' development ('we have a clearer view of what students actually require' and a 'deeper understanding of the needs of new entrants to the profession'), there were also many times that teachers needed to express their uncertainty. As Nias (1989) puts it, teaching is 'an occupation that is felt as well as experienced'. One recently qualified teacher felt intimidated by her two capable mature students, and asked if this could be changed next time. Another noted, 'my particular students did not make me feel confident – this has not happened before'. Many teachers said that they enjoyed their involvement but 'would like college to provide the theory'. Particularly early on, guidance was required over how to help the students' development or build up their responsibilities. As time went on often this was more to do with reassurance, so that tutor visits were awaited for confirmation. As a teacher said to me recently, 'Am I doing the right thing?' This need was expressed by requests: for more visits; for tutors to carry out more observations; for 'more discussion time about the progress of students in relation to first teaching experience expectations'.

Students, too, needed support. Often the best place for this was college territory, since there students felt less inhibited. Thus, two mature and, apparently, confident students visited me regularly over their serial placement to ask for advice over how to negotiate with their teacher, firstly over their workload, and then over their need for feedback, since they did not find 'oh you're doing fine' precise enough. They would then return to try out the strategies they had devised and 'clear the air' as they put it. After one such session one of them remarked, 'We practise on you first. We've devised our own assertiveness training course.' Part of this support was also through evaluation. Students saw the tutor as an assessor and wanted constructive feedback. 'Tutors understand when lessons are going wrong.' 'The most supportive factor was hearing tutors' opinions of your teaching.'

STUDENTS' PERSPECTIVES

The sense of entering what one student referred to as 'foreign territory', noted above, was a significant feature of student reactions. It was important to them that they were welcomed and made to feel wanted. The early induction programmes mentioned before, involving showing them round the school, explaining how to pay for tea and coffee, finding them somewhere to sit in the staffroom, and covering apparently trivial matters, were important in this respect. Of course, not every school has a staffroom big enough to accommodate extra people, but students note when they are being excluded, rather than there being a problem of space. Ways of including them as temporary members of the school staff varied from school to school. At one school they might have their own room for breaks, and thus have the privacy to 'get things off their chests', but not the opportunity to gain that insight into relationships that comes from observing a school staff at playtime. At another they might be included naturally in all activities from the birthday card list to planning for the Outward Bound weekend, or being invited to parties and teachers' homes.

Above all students appreciated the ways in which teachers took a serious interest in their training. 'It was wonderful that the class teacher had read her copy of the booklet and knew what was expected of us.' 'Support was excellent, they were always making themselves available for discussion about difficulties and putting their ideas forward.' Many teachers gave a lot of their time, helping students to evaluate sessions after school, brainstorming ideas, lending their own books and materials.

Managing stress

It is easy to forget how daunting school experience can appear to students at any stage, but especially in the first year, when a whole series of other adjustments are being made: living away from home for the first time; juggling the demands of one's own children with studying; making new relationships. While it is true that teaching is always stressful, on school experience this is compounded by novelty, intensity and uncertainty.

It is no wonder then, that a majority of the students, as well as depending on their tutor and teacher, turned to their partner for support. They commented: 'I wouldn't have been able to do it on my own', and 'a second person to bring the problems to was good; without that the stress would have been impossible'; or even: 'I might not have got through it without someone to talk to'. Commonly used emotion laden expressions in talking about this support were: 'comfort', 'encouragement', 'reassurance', 'boost in confidence', 'moral support'.

As these comments suggest, one way to relieve the stress was to talk through difficulties, particularly admitting weaknesses in a non-threatening situation away from teacher or tutor. 'I was able to talk over problems with my partner and felt better afterwards.' 'I learned to share problems more and not keep them to myself.' 'Having a partner gave you someone else in the same position as yourself with whom you could discuss your problems.' So that this person was also 'someone who had to go through the same things as you', and, as students discovered, 'she was just as anxious as me and that reassured me'.

Developing professional relationships

However, students realised that the support need not only be emotional. There was plenty of practical assistance within a developing professional relationship. In depending on someone else ('when you're in trouble your partner can help you out') they learnt the advantages of planning together, learning to co-operate, sharing their work 'and the load'. This notion of sharing appeared many times ('we learnt to share tasks evenly and not to let the other do the work or take over and do it myself') and was often accompanied by the words 'fairly' and 'equally', conveying the students' sense of justice and professional commitment in this arrangement. 'I could rely on my partner to do her fair share of the work.' Indeed those partners who were criticised were those who shirked their 'responsibility', left the work to their partner or were characterised as 'lazy' or unreliable; 'you can never get in touch with them to sort out problems'; 'they change their minds and only tell you that morning'.

Moreover, as developing professionals one's own feelings might sometimes have to be discounted in order to develop a working relationship: 'you learn to get on even when you're feeling irritable', and 'you forget personal feelings'. This sometimes involved the suppression of their own views ('you learn to bite your tongue'; 'you learn to be diplomatic'); learning to accept another's point of view ('I became more tolerant because of this'); and learning to compromise ('you don't have to agree all the time'). Students cited the following difficulties in gaining agreement: 'a disadvantage is when you think it's a good idea and your partner does not'; 'sometimes ideas clashed or when one person was teaching the partner would interrupt to put their view forward; this was very annoying'; 'students have different views of teaching, this led to arguments'. Yet they recognised that sometimes these disagreements have to be worked through: 'you had to work together to solve them'; 'you have to modify them to accommodate others'.

Communication

Students discovered that a key skill in working together, negotiating and resolving difficulties was communication. 'You have to learn to talk to each other', 'communication is essential'. It was a support in developing activities since 'you have double the ideas' and 'it was rewarding to share ideas'. But it is also essential for solving problems; 'we learnt to talk things through when we were not in agreement'. In doing so they became better listeners, 'even if this meant accepting someone else's idea was better than your own'.

Communication skills also developed in evaluating their lessons; 'we talked about every lesson' because 'it helped learning to be a better teacher'. The skill here became the ability to give and receive what was termed 'constructive criticism'. 'I listened to criticism without taking offence.' 'I learnt how to discuss honestly and openly.' 'I accepted criticism as a way of improving.' 'I have learnt how to tell my partner my honest opinion without seeming too critical.' Again this was often less threatening because of the equal relationship between students. A partner 'could give positive and negative points easier than the teacher or tutor.' Students

realised it was possible to do this without undermining their relationship. 'When a lesson didn't go too well I found it easier to talk
to my partner and I'm glad there was someone there to talk to
me.' At the same time this appeared to develop students' empathy, particularly 'the ability to respond to problems other than
your own'. 'I noticed the signs when the other was having problems and when it is appropriate to help.' As Stengelhofen says:
'Peer feedback is also important in laying down the concept that it
is part of professional work to be observed and evaluated by
one's own colleagues' (quoted in Fish, 1995: 129).

Like the teachers and tutors, students also needed to express
their uncertainties and insecurities. Automatically, some compared themselves unfavourably with their partner: 'you feel pressurised if you think your partner is doing better than you'. When
such fears are voiced they can be addressed, but sometimes, of
course, this does not happen and they eat away at the student's
self-confidence: 'you're not sure of whether you're capable of
teaching'. On the other hand it can be difficult to cope with another dominant personality without help: 'I was overshadowed
by a powerful partner'; 'I felt intimidated'; 'it was quite stressful
as my partner was quite dominant and I had to push myself to
speak up'.

Similarly, some students found it difficult to establish themselves because there might be several adults in the classroom, including the class teacher, their partner, a classroom assistant, and
perhaps a parent. 'It took longer to establish your personal identity in school because the children's attention was divided'; 'children not coming to you for help can be degrading'; 'you feel less
of an authority'. In fact, at times, it needed to be clear who was in
control: 'the children didn't know who the real teacher was'; 'too
many chiefs in the classroom, the children didn't know who was
in charge'. Once they were established and settled in a classroom
and the end of the experience was in sight some students longed
for independence and autonomy: 'there were long periods of in-
activity when I wanted to be teaching'; 'I sometimes wished I
could be *totally* in charge'. Ironically, when I visited some of them
on their second year practice, they were looking back nostalgic-
ally to the days when there was a shoulder to cry on, or someone
to dash to the photocopier for them. But these are aspects of partnership that they might develop with future colleagues, perhaps.

CONCLUSION

As I hope has become clear from this discussion, each of the participants has a complementary role. Teachers provide expertise in the practical context; tutors contribute institutional support, knowledge of research and the opportunity to reflect on practice in general, beyond specific contexts; students offer each other opportunities to develop skills in evaluation and professional relationships. Each has had to look at their role in a new way, and, moreover, learn to view situations from someone else's perspective: experienced practitioner and novice; established member of the community and outsider.

Several commentators have noted the fluency with which experienced teachers work, and which they 'tend to take for granted, not recognising the complexity of what they are doing, (which) can make teaching look misleadingly easy to novices' (Haggar *et al.*, 1993: 9). It is, therefore, important that this invisible expertise is made explicit, rather than it being assumed that somehow students will pick up the necessary skills along the way. Each of the participants, thus, has a role in focusing students' learning by capitalising on experiences and opportunities for observation and discussion. Some of the ways of doing this are set out in Appendix 1.

REFERENCES

DFE (Department for Education) (1992) *Initial Teacher Training (Secondary Phase)* (Circular 9/92), London: DFE.

Fish, D. (1995) *Quality Mentoring for Student Teachers,* London: Fulton.

Haggar, H., Burn, K. and McIntyre, D. (1993) *The School Mentor Handbook,* London: Kogan Page.

HMI (1991) *School-based Initial Teacher Training in England and Wales,* London: HMSO.

Jacques, K. (1993) 'Mentoring in initial teacher education', *Cambridge Journal of Education* 22 (3): 337–350.

Nias, I. (1989) *Primary Teachers Talking: A Study of Teaching as Work,* London: Routledge.

APPENDIX 1: PROVIDING SUPPORT

Experiences

As the chapter indicated, teachers are supportive in providing progressive experiences according to the experience and abilities of the students (as June did for Simon and Kathy). These may be by ensuring that:

- their first experiences are positive, so that they work, initially, with individuals and groups who are not seen as 'difficult' and teach in collaboration with experienced colleagues;
- there is a programme whereby they are introduced to the school and the way it works. Students need to know what the school expects of them, and other teachers need to know what students are expected to do and the pattern of their training over the placement.
- they have time to plan, observe and evaluate. Students can appear capable and confident but it is easy to forget they are not experienced. They have no bank of previous lessons to draw upon and they cannot observe and comment on children's learning in the same way as practised teachers. They need time to stand back and reflect.

Guided observation

Observation of teachers, peers and children is a common requirement of education courses. However, it can be difficult for students to see the benefits of it for several reasons, as Haggar *et al.* (1993: 38f.) point out:

- Sometimes a teacher's performance may be so fluent it is difficult to separate the different elements. It is 'an art that conceals art'.
- Students are working on the basis of what they already know. This might be insufficient to help them realise how complex teaching is.
- Very recently they may have been pupils themselves and continue to see the classroom from this point of view. They may not appreciate the amount of work that has gone on behind the scenes. They need to make the familiar strange.

- They may have preconceptions about the kind of teacher they are going to be ('I want to be a *natural* teacher'), or their own experiences and abilities ('I don't need a course on child development, I'm a mother'; 'I'm not one of these dependent eighteen year olds'). They can be, therefore, very judgemental, and even insensitive, about teachers who do not conform to these expectations.
- They may feel that learning to teach means working with the children all the time, not learning by observing the practice of others.

It follows, therefore, that the purpose of an observation and its focus should be clear:

- What preparation needs to take place beforehand? Will there be a discussion with the teacher/peer about the context of the lesson and her objectives?
- How will it be carried out? Will shorthand notes or an observation schedule be used?
- What will the focus be: questioning techniques; managing children; pacing and timing of lessons; responses of individual children?

Discussion

For observation to be valuable in developing students' thinking it should be followed by discussion. Here the skill of giving and receiving feedback is needed – what the students above called 'constructive criticism'. To do this several skills are needed:

- Asking positive questions which help listeners to expose their own practice, without them feeling criticised or undermined: 'Why did you ... Could you explain how ... Could you tell me ...?' These need to focus on what went well and why.
- Using open-ended questions which help listeners to reveal their thinking and allow them to comment and reflect.
- Using questions which focus on particular aspects of a lesson, are specific yet convey negative aspects in an objective and constructive way.
- Using eye contact and positive body language.
- Developing the ability to listen and not to interject, be confrontational, or react defensively.

- Using feedback constructively by allowing time to reflect on it, decide on a further course of action, and, if necessary not dwelling on it, if it appears negative.

APPENDIX 2: SCHOOL EXPERIENCE COMPETENCES

The first year students on this experience were required to keep their own profile document, recording the development of certain qualities and skills. To do this they were provided with a Catalogue of Competences as a guide, and asked to record evidence for them, in discussion with their teacher. These are presented here for scrutiny in the knowledge that no such list is perfect (this one has already been refined through feedback from teachers and students) but may sharpen our awareness.

Assessing students by means of discrete skills can appear 'superficially attractive but educationally flawed' (Fish, 1995: 150). Since there are no agreed criteria for drawing up such lists they can fail to account for many of the things that teachers do and, more particularly, why they do them. Competence, in the holistic sense, can be different from a collection of competences. As part of a profile they 'can reflect the personal and professional progress of the individual' (Fish, 1995: 165). These competences, therefore, are offered on the following basis:

- The students are encouraged to reflect on how they have carried them out and to add a written comment, not to regard them as a basic checklist to be ticked off.
- They are only one part of their personal assessment and are formative, not summative.
- One instance would not be sufficient evidence; a response would need to be made in several contexts.
- They are intended to guide the students' learning and their discussions with the teacher.

Catalogue of competences

Term one

- Shows an interest in children and relates to them as individuals.
- Explores school environment and procedures, takes opportunities presented to contribute to school life.
- Responds to professional demands of working in school including punctuality and personal and professional presentation.

Term two

- Takes account of the personal, social and emotional needs of children.
- Can prepare an activity for a group or class.
- Communicates sensitively and effectively with staff and parents.
- Uses a variety of teaching approaches.
- Seeks and acts on advice.
- Uses self-evaluation to improve professional skills.
- Presents material which provides for differences between children.
- Uses and manages a range of resources including AVA and IT.

Term three

- Can plan a sequence of work for a class of children.
- Uses displays as part of the teaching programme.
- Records children's learning in order to assist in planning the next stage.

8

COLLABORATING IN ASSESSMENT: THE OFSTED EXPERIENCE

Gill Hackett

THE SCHOOL'S VIEW

The dreaded buff envelope appears in the headteacher's post – the first indication to a school that the inspectors are coming! So after months, perhaps years, of anxious waiting this is finally 'it'! The official notification from Her Majesty's Chief Inspector of Schools informs the headteacher that an inspection will take place within the next year. There follows a further period of waiting until a date is agreed. In some ways this is the most stressful time of all for the senior management of a school. Clearly the period of advanced warning must be a time of preparation, but where and when to begin?

There is no purpose to be served by frantic activity. This only increases the tension which everyone must be feeling – after all the inspection may still be a year away. On the other hand, well planned and carefully executed preparations must surely be made. An opportunity is presented and if this time is well managed then staff are likely to approach the inspection in a more confident frame of mind.

The starting point for a school's preparation is, of necessity, *The OFSTED Handbook* containing the Inspection Schedule (OFSTED, 1995). This document was revised in 1995 and is readily available so that schools can be familiar in advance with the nature and scope of the inspection process and the criteria which will be employed. Schools will be aware that the final report must follow the structure and headings set out in the Inspection Schedule:

1 Main findings
2 Key issues for action
3 Characteristics of the school

143

Key indicators

4 Educational standards achieved by pupils at the school:

- Attainment and progress
- Attitudes, behaviour and personal development
- Attendance

5 Quality of education provided:

- Teaching
- The curriculum and assessment
- Spiritual, moral, social and cultural development
- Support, guidance and pupils' welfare
- Partnerships with parents and the community

6 The management and efficiency of the school:

- Leadership and management
- Staffing, accommodation and learning resources
- The efficiency of the school

7 Areas of learning for children under five
8 English, mathematics and science
9 Other subjects of the curriculum

While the senior staff of a school are likely to be in the best position to identify issues which need to be addressed, few schools go into the inspection process unaided. Most Local Education Authorities deploy their own inspection staff to act as advisers to schools and a number of independent consultancies also offer advice. As experienced inspectors themselves, these people are well placed to help schools in their preparation. Schools are often concerned about the amount of paperwork they will be asked to produce prior to the inspection. Much of this can be assembled well in advance, avoiding last minute panics. Schools are discouraged, however, from undertaking the burden of producing vast quantities of new policies or other documents simply for the inspection.

All teachers are aware that during an inspection they can expect to have a considerable number of their lessons observed by an inspector who will be making copious notes. This can be a very stressful experience and some schools take steps, during this preparatory period, to minimise the fear of observation by having 'dry runs'. The criteria which will inform lesson observations are clearly stated in the Inspection Schedule and teachers will have time to become familiar with them and to know how their lessons will be assessed. Opportunities are given in some schools for staff to observe and be observed with subsequent opportunities for professional discussion. In this way teachers may feel active in reviewing and developing their own professional skills and are also less likely to feel threatened by the presence of an inspector.

In parallel with the period of preparation in schools, the pre-inspection process continues. Following the announcement of a 'batch' of schools, bids are invited from inspection bodies to carry out the inspection. These bids must identify members of proposed teams, as consideration of their suitability and experience is an important factor in the awarding of contracts. An experienced Registered Inspector to lead the inspection must be nominated plus a number of team members who possess the necessary professional experience and expertise to cover between them all aspects of the inspection. A Lay Inspector must also be named.

AN INSPECTOR'S VIEW

The number of teachers who experience an OFSTED inspection multiplies each term and each will have a different perception of what was involved. Clearly, teachers' perceptions, viewing the workings of a team from the outside, will be different from those operating from within it. My own perspective is that of a primary team inspector. Each inspection is unique in many ways, reflecting the differences between schools, but there is also a consistency which is guaranteed by application of the Inspection Schedule. To some extent every inspection is also different because each Registered Inspector brings his or her own style and ways of working, yet each is the same in that set procedures and criteria must be employed. What follows is a team inspector's eye view of a primary school inspection which is typical of many.

I work with only one inspection unit as my post in higher education allows me to be involved in only a limited number of inspections each year. Having agreed in advance those weeks when I can be available, my next communication regarding this inspection arrives when a bid has been successful and dates are confirmed. At this point I am told the name of the school and of the RgI (Registered Inspector). I also hear that I am to be responsible for the inspection of two curriculum areas and for the co-ordination of evidence relating to the quality of provision for and standards achieved by pupils with special educational needs. I am told that I am the core team inspector. As such I will have some additional responsibilities in support of the RgI. This will mean attending both the pre-inspection meeting for parents and also the post-inspection meetings with the senior management team of the school and with the governors. During the inspection I must be prepared to undertake additional work if necessary to support the RgI and I can expect to be involved in the proof reading and possibly the redrafting of the report. Although the extra demands are considerable, I welcome this role as it gives me a greater feeling of involvement and of a coherent process.

During the weeks leading up to the inspection I need to ensure that I am thoroughly prepared. I spend time reading and re-considering the National Curriculum documentation (DFE, 1995) for the curriculum areas for which I am responsible. I also revisit *The OFSTED Handbook*, looking particularly at those areas I shall inspect. I make sure that I read any additional guidance produced by OFSTED. Teachers in the school are preparing thoroughly for the inspection and I know I owe it to them to be just as well pre-pared. At this stage, however, the preparation is general in nature. It cannot focus specifically on the school until a few weeks before the inspection date.

Two weeks in advance of the inspection, the detailed documen-tation regarding the school begins to arrive. Some documents will be received by all team members and others will go only to the particular inspector who needs to see it. All inspectors will re-ceive copies of the following documents:

- The PICSI (Pre-inspection Context and School Indicator report) which contains information derived from the most recent census and provides quantitative information about the social and economic characteristics of the area in which the school is situated.
- The Headteacher's form which contains detailed information about the school itself, numbers, attendance, organisation, staffing, the curriculum and financial matters.
- The school prospectus and staff handbook.
- A plan of the school.
- Timetables for the inspection week.

In addition I receive the policy documents for those inspection areas for which I am responsible. At this stage detailed preparation must begin as some pre-inspection documentation must be produced.

For each of these areas inspectors must produce a Pre-Inspection Commentary and a set of Issues for Inspection. These will form part of the total inspection evidence which must be submitted to OFSTED. Examination of the documentation I have received enables relevant points to be identified. This pre-inspection procedure highlights issues for inspection and raises hypotheses about the school which will be followed up during the course of the inspection. Identification of issues at this stage does not preclude the possibility of other issues arising during the week. During the inspection further evidence will be gathered which will confirm, extend or modify this preliminary analysis.

My other task is to prepare a draft timetable for myself for the four days of inspection. At least 60 per cent of an inspector's time in school must be spent in direct classroom observation – in practice it is usually considerably more. I must ensure that I am able to observe the teaching of my two curriculum areas in as representative a way as possible. I need to see all ages and ability groups and I shall want to see the postholder 'in action'. This proves difficult to plan as some subjects are timetabled at the same time for every class and sufficient time must be spent in each lesson to feel confident about the judgements I have to make. Once completed I know this timetable is only provisional until we meet as a team and cross-check with each other to ensure that there is adequate coverage without undue overload to individuals. In addition to classroom observation I shall need time to interview postholders, examine resources and look at pupils' work.

WORKING AS A TEAM

In the week preceding the inspection there is a team meeting followed by the meeting for parents. Some RgIs hold the preliminary meeting immediately before the inspection starts but I find this earlier meeting helpful to establish a team feeling and approach. In addition to the RgI there are three professional team members, including myself, and a lay inspector. None of us has worked together before, though most are very experienced. For one member it is her first inspection. We need to establish good working relationships quickly as much of the success of the inspection depends upon the trust we have in each other's professional judgements. The RgI reminds us of the Code of Conduct for Inspectors which is to be found in *The OFSTED Handbook*. We aim to be professional but approachable, trying to make the week no more uncomfortable than it has to be for the school. We hope that staff will feel genuinely involved in the process and that we are prepared to discuss issues with them as they arise.

As core team member I must also attend the parents' meeting with the RgI. This meeting has been convened by the governing body and is only open to parents of children in the school. Prior to the meeting they have received a standard form inviting responses and the RgI has data from the returns. The headteacher will introduce us and then withdraw. She appears friendly, though understandably a little tense. The RgI has already visited the school and talked to her and also the staff and governors. This is an important stage in the process and seems to me to be crucial to the smooth running of the inspection. The RgI has been able to explain the process and answer questions. He has talked about the team members and their responsibilities and has reassured everyone that our background and experience is appropriate. These meetings will have set the tone for the inspection.

The parents' meeting is sparsely attended, perhaps a sign that the majority are satisfied with what the school provides. The RgI outlines the inspection process and the purpose of the meeting. It is, he explains, their opportunity to raise issues or questions with the inspection team. He wishes to seek their views about the school and these will be noted though not commented upon at this stage. The meeting follows a set agenda and is generally very supportive of the head and staff. The atmosphere is good. The RgI clearly shows that he values parents' opinions. They seem reassured. The headteacher is waiting for us at the close of the meeting and over coffee the RgI shares with her the main points which have emerged from the questionnaire and this evening's meeting. She is able to respond in this informal setting and I can see that she and the RgI are already establishing a good working relationship.

The inspection is scheduled to take place over four days and the team assembles at the school by eight o'clock on the first morning. This will be the pattern for each day. The school has set aside a spare classroom for our use and we are able to gather the observation forms which will be needed during the day. Timetables are then co-ordinated. In primary schools, particularly small ones, the pressure of being observed can be very great and the RgI is sensitive to the need to ensure, if possible, that every teacher has some time each day free from the presence of an inspector. In order to be confident in our judgements about reading we decide to sample 10 per cent of the pupils in the school. This will involve all team members, not just the inspector with responsibility for English who has produced guidance which all will follow. We shall encourage pupils to talk about their attitudes to reading and choice of books as well as hearing them read aloud and discussing the texts. Team members briefly share first impressions of the school and the inspection begins in earnest. One inspector departs to watch pupils arriving and make notes about supervision, others prepare to attend assembly or have a first walk round the school.

It is at this stage that the accumulation of the bulk of the inspection evidence begins. All judgements in the final report must be based on a substantial evidence base which is systematically collected and analysed. This evidence will be gathered by:

- observation of lessons;
- scrutiny of pupils' work;
- discussion with pupils;
- discussion with teachers, governors, parents and others involved in the work of the school;
- review of documentary evidence.

For the first day we are engaged in intensive lesson observation. Observation made in lessons constitutes the major evidence for judgements about the quality of teaching and learning in the school. For every lesson, or part of a lesson, that is observed, an observation form must be completed. On this form the inspector records judgements about pupils' attainment and progress and about the quality of the teaching that is being observed. An overall grading for the lesson must also be awarded. At the end of the inspection these grades form an important part of the evidence base, though they must not be viewed as definitive indicators and have to be considered alongside other evidence before arriving at judgements.

The school seems well prepared. In each classroom a chair is ready for an inspector's visit and a planning file has been placed upon it. This is helpful and minimises the disruption my presence

GILL HACKETT

may cause. I look closely at the lesson plan each time. I am able to see the teacher's aims and objectives for the lesson, what s/he aims to cover and how s/he will organise learning for the range of pupils in the class. These are factors which will be important in making a judgement about the quality of the teaching. Observation gives me insights into the effectiveness with which the plans are carried out. I will be asking myself questions such as:

• Is the teaching purposeful, does it create interest and motivation?
• Is the lesson managed in an orderly way?
• How effective are the interactions between teacher and pupils?

In judging the effectiveness of the teaching, the responses of pupils to tasks and resources are crucial and time must be spent not only in looking at their work and observing their approaches and attitudes, but also in talking to them to ascertain their understanding of what they are doing. I must try to determine the level of match between the tasks and the pupils' needs. When considering standards which are being achieved the criteria for inspection require two judgements to be made. I must consider the attainment of pupils in each curriculum area in relation to national standards and expectations but must also identify the progress pupils are making in relation to their prior attainment. These are difficult judgements to make and I am very conscious of the need to be fair and objective. Each of these aspects of the lesson must be graded and a scale of one to seven is used. Where there is insufficient evidence for a judgement to be made 0 is recorded.

While pupils are busily occupied with tasks it is sometimes possible to have a brief conversation with the teacher. When I am able to do so this is useful as I am able to ask about particular children or aspects of their work. This helps me to make a more informed assessment of the standards which are being achieved. I can share with the class teacher some of my observations and invite comments. In some lessons another adult is working in the classroom in a support role. Time must be taken for discussion with these staff or volunteers as well as for observation of the contribution they are making to the learning environment. As far as possible I aim to see a whole lesson, though in longer sessions it is sometimes possible to carry out two separate observations. In any case it is essential to spend long enough in a lesson to feel confident about my judgements. At the end of the lesson I try not to leave the room before having a brief conversation with the teacher. This must not involve revealing judgements but gives me an opportunity to engage in a professional conversation which will generally make supportive comments as well as raise issues. We may, for example, discuss the choice of activity or resources or consider the method of organisation employed. The rigorous format of the observation form may be known but by these brief conversations I can try to minimise the anxiety of a stressful situation as well as gain insights into the teacher's thinking.

Evidence relating to provision for pupils with special educational needs and their attainment is gathered throughout the week. Colleagues will be considering this aspect of the inspection process as they observe lessons in each curriculum area, evaluating the quality of the provision and the progress made by pupils. Samples of work will be carefully scrutinised and we shall ensure that we talk to these pupils and their teachers. As I have responsibility for co-ordinating this aspect of the inspection I shall receive written evidence from the other inspectors and I shall have to interview the SENCO and examine the school's procedures and documentation. By the end of the inspection we must reach a corporate judgement to insert into the report.

At the end of the first day we have our team meeting. We have to ensure that all observation forms are passed to the RgI who will be checking and collating them on a daily basis. The first day is reviewed. At this point the task still seems overwhelming! Already, however, we are beginning to get a corporate 'feel' for the school though judgements must remain very tentative at this stage. The RgI has had several conversations with the headteacher during the day and arrangements have been made for us to interview postholders at assembly times during the next two days.

The interviews with postholders must be carefully planned. Some staff will be interviewed several times by different inspectors and sensitivity is needed. A number of issues for discussion were identified in the pre-inspection commentaries and, having spent time in the school, there are now other points I wish to discuss with the relevant members of staff. I want to ensure that I find out all I need to know from each postholder at this stage so that, unless unexpected issues arise, I will not need to ask for any more of their time. I hope that as far as possible these interviews can be dialogues and can be conducted in a non-threatening way. I encourage staff to describe their roles to me and give them opportunities to highlight strengths both in their own work and in the school's achievements. On each occasion these turn out to be very useful discussions. My questions are answered and, where I have raised concerns, I have seen that staff are often aware of difficulties and are able to describe steps they are taking. We are able to share ideas about possible ways forward. I record all details of the interviews.

By the end of the second day a substantial bank of evidence has been accumulated. Several hours are now spent in scrutinising pupils' work. A range of work from all classes and abilities in all areas of the curriculum has been assembled, together with reports and pupil records. The evidence which is gathered from this exercise is very significant and complements evidence from observations. Here we are able to see work over a period of time, adding not only to our judgement of standards but also to our perceptions of the breadth and balance of the curriculum. We are also able to examine in depth the systems for recording and reporting pupil progress.

At the start of the third day, as timetables are reviewed, it is clear that the burden of observation is falling more heavily on some staff than others and the RgI insists that changes are made accordingly. As on each morning, we are told if there are areas where the body of inspection evidence is light and we are directed to give them additional attention. Timetabling constraints have made it difficult for there to be adequate observation of science teaching so far, so we rearrange our timetables to cover more science lessons. In this way team members support each other in the gathering of evidence.

During the course of this day I spend time examining the school's resources for the teaching of the curriculum areas for which I am responsible. I have seen some of these in evidence in the classrooms and considered the ways in which they are used. Now I look closely at the full range of materials that is available. This includes books and other published materials, but I shall also look at the computers and software available to develop information technology capability.

At the end of the third day or on the final day, at times which are convenient to the staff, each of us will give brief oral feedback to the postholders so that they are aware in general terms of what will be said in the relevant parts of the report. At this stage there is still time for evidence to be offered if anything has been missed and for any factual inaccuracies to be clarified. In this way staff are encouraged to feel part of the process and to see their contributions as important. Their professional status in the school is also recognised in this acknowledgement that they should be first to know the inspection judgements relating to areas for which they are responsible.

It is at the end of this third day that thoughts turn explicitly to the substance of the final report. The RgI has asked team members to prepare their draft judgements and comments and these are formally shared. We have collated our own evidence and now ensure that we receive all relevant comments from the rest of the team. The agenda for the meeting is to go through the format of the Record of Evidence and discuss corporate judgements and grades to be given. It is clear from the discussion that the team has gathered a wealth of information in a short time. Where evidence is still incomplete there is an opportunity to supplement it on the final day of the inspection. By the time of the final meeting on the following day all evidence must be in place so that the report findings can then be agreed.

At the end of the final inspection day, while staff are breathing a sigh of relief, and, hopefully, breaking open the sparkling wine and passing round the cream cakes, the inspection team meets for its final and most important meeting.

From the enormous amount of evidence which has been accumulated we must decide those sections of the final report which will be included under the headings: Main Findings and Key Issues for Action. The Inspection Schedule states that:

> The main findings should reflect the essential characteristics and qualities of the school. They should focus on the educational standards achieved by pupils and the strengths and weaknesses in the quality of education provided, especially teaching, and on the management and efficiency of the school as they affect the standards.
>
> (OFSTED, 1995: 47)

There are many points we want to make. They have to be brainstormed onto a flipchart so that we can begin to prioritise them and decide what are the crucial findings of the inspection week. We want to ensure that we highlight the strengths and achievements of the school as well as identifying areas for development. It is several hours before we are confident of our decisions as we struggle not only with the substance of our ideas but also to find exactly the right words with which to express them. There is no attempt to hurry the process. No one is prepared to leave until we have achieved a result that we believe to be honest and fair and which reflects the judgements of us all.

Our final task is to tidy our room and depart, leaving no evidence of the presence that has dominated the school for a week. It is the last time we shall meet as a team. Five people who at the start of the week were strangers but who quickly forged into a coherent working unit.

But the work is not yet finished. Over the following days team members must formally complete inspection evidence forms and contribute key inspection evidence and findings for their areas of responsibility. Once again there will be agonising over words to express oneself clearly and concisely. The final task of writing the report, redrafting contributions and ensuring a coherent whole, falls to the Registered Inspector. RgIs must follow the structure specified in the Inspection Schedule and write in jargon-free language which will clearly communicate to both professional and non-professional readers. He or she must ensure that the report is internally consistent, that the judgements reflect the body of evidence and that the Main Findings and Key Issues for Action clearly arise from the judgements.

The OFSTED Handbook requires that as soon as possible the RgI shares the main findings of the report with the headteacher and any members of staff s/he wishes to invite to the meeting. On the morning following the inspection, therefore, I accompany the RgI to a meeting with the senior management team of the school. Here we present an oral summary of the report, including the Main Findings and Key Issues for Action. This is an opportunity to check the factual accuracy of the report before its completion. Judgements reached by the team cannot, however, be modified unless they are based on factual inaccuracies. The on-going conversations of the week have ensured that there are no surprises for the head and her staff. She and the RgI have had daily meetings about the progress of the inspection and other staff have been involved with many conversations with members of the team. They are pleased to see their strengths acknowledged and are already generally aware of the issues to be addressed. The meeting is courteous and professional.

Our final draft report is also taken to the closing meeting of the inspection which is with the governing body. This, too, is an oral reporting back, though copious notes are taken. The inspection findings are presented clearly and concisely, and governors are assured that there will be no substantive changes when the final report is published. Responsibility for addressing the Key Issues rests with the governors and at their next meeting they will begin to develop their action plan.

For me the inspection process is now almost complete. I have submitted my contributions to the report, though as core team inspector I know that I must expect to be involved in the redrafting stage and a few days later I receive drafts of the final report for comment.

For the school, however, the process continues. The action plan must be implemented. There will be some members of staff who will be engaged in a considerable amount of work for, although individuals are not named in the report, specific curriculum areas have been identified.

SCHOOL DEVELOPMENT

Only each individual school can say whether or not the inspection has been a positive experience. Despite the pressure caused, many schools who, like this one, approach inspection in a positive way find that it does have considerable benefits for them. The preparation period has been used to identify strengths and weaknesses and staff have grown accustomed both to analysing their own practice and engaging in professional discussion about it. The period of the inspection allowed for conversations with professionals who were able to offer an outsider's view and this was seen not as a threat but as an opportunity for further development. The Key Issues for Action which will be reflected on the governors' action plan can now be viewed in a positive light as showing the way forward to enhance the learning of the pupils in the school.

Is this too optimistic a view? Perhaps it is, but it certainly seemed to be reflected in this particular inspection where both the preparation and attitude of the school and the approach of the Registered Inspector and his team combined for maximum effect.

Where this is seen to be the case then the potential of inspection as a collaborative process would seem to be enhanced. It is to be hoped that, as inspection cycles become a permanent fixture in the life of a school, confidence will build between all parties so that, rather than viewing teachers and inspectors as being on opposite sides, we can work together for the benefit of children.

REFERENCES

DFE (Department for Education) (1995) *Key Stages 1 and 2 of the National Curriculum,* London: HMSO.
OFSTED (1995) *The OFSTED Handbook. Guidance on the Inspection of Nursery and Primary Schools,* London: HMSO.

INDEX

Note: Page numbers in **bold** type indicate references to case studies.
Abbreviations used in subheadings: SEN . . . special educational needs

accountability **16**, 34
Acker, S. 14
Ada, A.F. 88
agencies: collaboration on children with SEN 49, 58; collaboration with nursery schools **22–3**, **28–9**; coordination with 51–2; in environmental education **108**, 109–10
Agenda 21, Earth Summit 110
Allexsaht-Snider, M. 89
art **45**, 60, **106**; artists in residence **22**, **106**; in nursery schools **16**, **22**
Ashley Community School **24–9**
assessment, school 143–56
assistants *see* classroom assistants
Association for Science Education (ASE) 114
Association for Teacher Education in Europe (ATEE) 111
Audit Commission, reports on provision for SEN 62
Avon Schools Link International 112–13

Babington-Smith, B. and Farrell, B. 52
Balshaw, M. 54, 57, 61
Barnardo's **22**
Beddis, R. and Mares, C. 112, 113
Belfield Project 86, 96

Biott, C. and Easen, P. 6, 7
Birmingham Association for Environmental Education (BAEE) **109**
Birmingham Brazil Friendship Link 111
Birmingham Development Education Centre **107**, 109–10
Birmingham Environmental Planning **108**
Boulton Primary School, Handsworth **107–9**
Brandt Report (1980) 101
Brighouse, T. and Moon, B. 6
Bruner, L.S. 68

CAFOD 110
Caldwell, B.J. and Spinks, J.M. 38, 39
case studies in environmental education **105–9**; in initial teacher training **126–37**; in nursery education **13–29**; in revision of project cycle **40–5**, **46–7** (Appendices); in support for minority language families **93–4**, **95–7**
Centre of the Earth **109**
change, management of 33–7, 46
Child Care Strategy Committee **22**
children: collaboration with peers

68, 72–4, 80, 81; and parents and other adults 74–80, 85–98; partnerships in environmental education **105–7**; partnerships for literacy 67–8, 69–72, 74–80, 85–7; and teachers 67–8, 69–72
Children Act (1989) 1, 4, **20, 23**
Children and Teachers Talking Science (CHATTS) 114
Christian Aid 110
classroom assistants 3–4, 52, 53–7, 59, 61–2; effective use of 54–7, 62; for language support 3–4, **93**, **97**; and nursery nurses 53–4; and pupils with SEN 3, 52, 53–6; and teachers 53–6, 61–2; training of 53–4, 59, 60, 61–2
classroom work: adults other than teachers in 3–4, 53–62; changes 1–2; organisation in nursery work **16–17**; organisation for reading 69–72, 73–4, 77–9; withdrawal of children 60, 80
Clay, M.M. 70, 77, 78–9
Code of Conduct for Inspectors (OFSTED) 148
Code of Practice on the Identification and Assessment of Special Educational Needs (1994) **16**, 50
collaboration: 'culture of collaboration' 5–6; government initiatives in 4–6; with minority language families 87–93; in nursery education **13–29**; in planning 36–9; in school assessment 143–56; schools and outside agencies **22–3**, **28–9**, 51–2, 58, 109–10; *see also* partnership; relationships
communication inter-agency **23**, **29**; international environmental 113–14; in nursery education **14**, **15–17**, **20–1**, **26–7**; student development of **136–7**
community links **21–4**, **28–9**, **104**, **107**
competences, students' 141–2 (Appendix)

conditions of work 37
Council for Environmental Education (CEE) 110
Council of Europe 111
'culture of collaboration' 5–6, 30
Cummins, J. 92
curriculum: environmental education in 102–3; planning **16**, 36–9; revising a project cycle **40–5**, **46–7** (Appendices); trauma of changes in 33–4; *see also* National Curriculum

David, T. 4, 23
Dearing, Sir Ron and Dearing Report 34, 102–3
De'Athe, E. and Pugh, G. 8
democracy, and children 115–18
developing countries 111–13

e-mail 112, 113–14
Earth Summit (1992) 101, 110, 111
Easen, P. *see* Biott, C. and Easen, P.
ECO Environmental Education Trust 116
Education Acts: (1981) 3, 4, 48; (1986) 4; (1988) 4, 14; (1993) 48
Education (Handicapped Children) Act (1970) 49
educational psychologists 50, 51
Elliott, J. 6
empowerment of children 101–2, 113, 117–18
English Nature **105**, **108**
environmental education 100–18, 120–2(Appendices); aims 101–2; case histories **105–9**, **120–2** (Appendices); children's approach to 114–18; in curriculum 102–3; entry points for action 104–5; networking outside school **107**, **108**, 109–14; in school 103–9
Environmental Education into Initial Training in Europe (EEITE) 111
ESSO 110
ethnic minorities, and literacy 3–4, **28**, 87–98

European Community (EC), and environmental education 110–11

Family Literacy Project 95
Farrell, B. *see* Babington-Smith, B. and Farrell, B.
financial resources 33, 35–6
Fish, D. 127, 129, 141
Fox, G. 61
Framework for Inspection 145
Friends of the Earth 104
Fullan, M. 35–6, 37

geography **40**, **45**, **106**
Global Futures Project (WWF) 115
government initiatives: in educational collaboration 4–6; in forcing change 36, 37
Green Letter Filter Service 110
'greening' school environment **105–7**, **108–9**
Greenlink 110
Greig, S. *et al.* 104–5
GRIDS **15**
group reading 68, 69–72, 80, 81

Haggar, H. *et al* 131, 133, 138, 139
Hannon, P. 96
Hargreaves, D. 1, 6
Haringey Project 86, 87–8, 96
headteachers: fostering leadership 38, 39; in nursery education 13, **14–16**, **18–19**, **24**; in school inspection 146, 148, 151, 154–5
health services **22–3**, **28–9**, 49
Her Majesty's Inspectorate (HMI): Code of Conduct for Inspectors (OFSTED) 148; and provision for SEN 62, 145–6, 151; Registered Inspectors (RgI) 145, 147–8, 152, 153, 154–5; *School-based Initial Teacher Education* (1991) 125; *see also* inspection
Hicks, D. 115
history 33, **40**, **45**, **106**
home visits 86, 87, **95–7**
home-language storytelling **92**

Huckle, J. 102

industry, links with **23–4**, 110
information technology **44**, **45**, **108**, 113–14, 152
inspection 143–56; effect on school development 155–6; final report 153–5; Framework for Inspection 145, 154; headteacher's involvement 146, 148, 151, 154–5; Inspection Schedule 143–5, 153; inspection team and teamwork 147–55; inspectors' preparation for 145–9; parents' involvement in 147–8; procedure followed 149–55; school preparations for 143–5, 149–50
inspectors *see* Her Majesty's Inspectorate (HMI); inspection
inter-school linkages **21–2**, **107**, **109**, 111–13
International Centre for Conservation Education (ICCE) 110
international linkages, in environmental education **107**, **109**, 111–14

Jacques, K. 130, 132
Jungnitz, G. 90

Keep, R. 113
Kings Norton Primary School, Birmingham **105–7**, **120–2** (Appendices)

Labour Party Education Policy, *Diversity and Excellence: A New Partnership for Parents* (1995) 1
language: home-language storytelling **92**; language support 3–4, **22**, **28**, **93**, **95**, **97**; minority language families 87–98; multilingual schools 3–4, **28**, 87–9
leadership 38–9, 46, 58, 103
learning, as social process 68
Learning through Landscape **109**

literacy 67–82, 84–98, **89–90**;
  Belfield Project 86, 96; forms of
  collaboration in 67–82;
  Haringey study 86, 87–8, 96;
  strategies for minority language
  families 84–98, **89–90**; *see also*
  reading
Local Education Authority
  (LEA): Environmental Studies
  Centre **108**; support from **21–2**,
  49, 144

MacConville, R. 55–6
Mares, C. *see* Beddis, R. and
  Mares, C.
Marris, P. 36–7
Meadows, J.J. 113
Moon, B. *see* Brighouse, T. and
  Moon, B.
Moseley CE Junior School 115

National Association for
  Environmental Education
  (NAEE) **109**, 110
National Curriculum 6, 34, **40–2**,
  43–4; and environmental
  education 102–3; on literacy 69;
  and school inspection 146; *see*
  also curriculum
National Foundation for
  Educational Research 3–4
National Primary Centre project
  21
nature trails **105**, **108**
Neal, P. *see* Palmer, J. and Neal, P.
networking 52, 53, 100–18, 120–2
  (Appendices); developing
  countries 111–13;
  environmental agencies 109–10;
  in environmental education
  100–18, 120–2 (Appendices); in
  Europe 110–11; outside school
  109–14, 120–2 (Appendices)
Newsom Report (1963) 2
Nias, J. 30, 133
Norton School, Cheshire 113
nursery education 13–30
nursery nurses **18**, **19**, **22**, 53–4
nursery vouchers 4

observation: by HMI 144–5, 147,
  149–51, 152; by student teachers
  139–40 (Appendix); of student
  teachers **128–30**
OFSTED: guidelines for nursery
  schools **16**; *Handbook* 143–4, 146;
  and school assessment
  inspections 143–57
'open door' policy **19**, **20**
OPTIS 61

Palmer, J. 113–14
Palmer, J. and Neal, P. 103
parents: and children's literacy
  74–5, 79, 85–98; involvement
  with school 2–5, 8, 58, **94**, **105–6**;
  meeting with inspection teams
  147–8; in minority language
  families 87–98; in nursery
  education **19–21**, **27–9**; and
  teachers 86–9, 93–4
Parents' Charter (DES, 1991) 4–5
Parkway Nursery School **13–24**,
  31–2 (Appendices)
Parry, M.L. 100
partnership 1–8, 125; with
  minority language families
  84–98; in nursery education
  13–30; in reading 67–82;
  school-based training schemes
  125–38, 139–42 (Appendices); *see*
  also collaboration; relationships
peer tutoring 68, 72–4, 80, 81
Pied Crow primary school
  environmental magazine,
  Kenya 113
planning: in nursery education
  14–17, **25–7**, **31** (Appendix); in
  primary education 33–46; vision
  in 38–9
pollution 114–15, 117
postholders 33, **42–3**, 147,
  151–3
Poulton, P. and Symons, G. 103
project cycle revision case study
  40–5, **46–7** (Appendices)

reading 67–82, 84–98, 149;
  book-related support **90–1**;

group reading 68, 69–72, 80, 81; and home-language storytelling 92; inspection assessment 149; in local community languages 92; for meaning 68, **89, 90**; paired reading 68, 74–7, 80–1; partnerships in 67–82; peer tutoring 68, 72–4, 80, 81; provision of materials **92–3**; for pupils with SEN 59–60, 61; Reading Recovery schemes 68, 77–80, 81; sibling support **90**; *see also* literacy

Registered Inspectors (RgI) 145, 147–8, 152, 153, 154–5

relationships: designated as partnerships 7–8; development of professional **135–6**; flatter hierarchy in **17–19**, 58; international **107, 109**, 110–13; in nursery education **17–19, 26**; time taken in developing 56–7; *see also* collaboration; partnership

resources: equipment 152; financial 35–6; time **42**, 46, 57, 62

Royal National Institute for the Blind 49

Royal Society for the Protection of Birds (RSPB) 110

Save the Children Fund 116

Sayco **23**

school development, and inspection 155–6

School Development Plans: 'culture of collaboration' 5–6, 30; and environmental education 103–4, **106–7, 108–9**; nursery school 14–17

School Watch 110

school-based partnership training schemes 125–38, 139–42 (Appendices); context **126**; students' perspectives of **134–7**; teachers' perspectives of **126–30**; tutors' perspectives of **130–4**

schools: Ashley Community School **24–9**; Boulton Primary School, Handsworth 107–9; Kings Norton Primary School, Birmingham **105–7, 120–2** (Appendices); Moseley CE Junior School 115; Norton School, Cheshire 113; Parkway Nursery School **13–24, 31–2** (Appendices)

science 33, **40**, 57, **94, 106**; outside consultants **44, 45**

Skilbeck, M. 6

special educational needs (SEN) **20**, 48–62, 145–6, 151; 1994 Code of Practice **16**, 50; classroom assistants 3, 52, 53–6; co-ordinator (SENCO) 50, 58; modification for **108**; and school inspection 145–6, 151; statements and assessment 50, 58, 59; teamwork 50–3, 56–7, 58–62; withdrawal from classroom 60

Spinks, J.M. *see* Caldwell, B.J. and Spinks, J.M.

staff *see* classroom assistants; headteachers; nursery nurses; student teachers; teachers

Stengelhofen, J. 137

stress: student **134–5**; teacher 37, 144–5

student teachers: commitment of **127, 128–9, 135**; perspective of school-based training **134–7**; relationship with partner **126, 135, 136–7**; relationship with teachers **127–30, 132–4**; in school-based training 125–38, 139–42 (Appendices); and tutors **131–4**; *see also* teachers

support: parental **20–1**, 85–9, **95–7**; in school-based teacher training **133–6**, 139–42 (Appendix)

Symons, G. *see* Poulton, P. and Symons, G.

Tbilisi Recommendations (1980) 101

teachers: and classroom assistants

53–6, 61–2; impact of change on 34–7; involvement in project planning **40–5**; learning support 51; nursery **18–19**, **25–6**; and nursery nurses **19**; outside advisory **44**; and parents 86–9, 93–4; and SEN teams 49, 50–62; and student teachers **127–30**, **132–4**; and tutors 132–3; *see also* student teachers

Teachers in Development Education (TIDE) 109

teaching materials: in environmental education 109–10, 116; for minority language students 3–4, **92–3**

team-teaching 3

teams and teamwork 52, 53; and HMI inspection 147–55; and SEN 50–3, 58–62

technology **40**, **45**, **108**

therapists **22**, **28**, 49, 51

Thomas, G. 7, 57

Thomas, L. *see* Timberlake, L. and Thomas, L.

Tidy Britain 110

Timberlake, L. and Thomas, L. 114–15

time: for adapting to change 36–7, **41–2**; in environmental curriculum 115; as scarce resource **42**, 46, 57, 62; to develop collaboration 56–7

Topping, K.J. 73

Topping, K.J. and Wolfendale, S.W. 74

training: in environmental education 104, 110–11; in inter-agency collaboration **22**,

29; for Reading Recovery 77; school-based partnership schemes 125–38, 139–42 (Appendices); for SEN classroom assistants 59, 60, 61–2

tutors: peers as 68, 72–4, 80, 81; in school-based training schemes **130–4**

UNICEF 116; *Rescue Mission Planet Earth* 115–16

United Nations: *Children and the Environment* (1990) 114; Intergovernmental Conference on Environmental Education (1977) 101

United Nations Environmental Programme (UNEP): *Good Earth Keeping* 116

vandalism **106–7**

vision, and leadership 38–9

Vygotsky, L. 72

Warnock Report (DES, 1978) 3, 48–9

Waterland, L. 75

Wells, C.G. 68

Westhill College 125

whole school approach 6, 33, **42–3**, 103–4

Wolfendale, S.W. *see* Topping, K.J. and Wolfendale, S.W.

World Commission on Environment and Development 101

World Wide Fund for Nature 104, 110, 116; Global Futures Project 115